MINIMALIST

BUDGET

How to use minimalism in your favor to finally get your finances in order and achieve the lifestyle of your dreams.

by Valentina Palermo V.

TABLE OF CONTENT

Introduction..5

Before we Start..11

What has Minimalism got to do with Budgeting........18

Income..22

Expenses...29

Assets...37

Liabilities...43

Net Worth..47

Cashflow..49

Debt...52

Lifestyle & Goals...58

Mindset & Habits..64

How to increase your Income................................74

Should I Get a Job or Start a Business?....................98

Rent vs Buy..102

Savings..107

Making a Budget...113

Budgeting Tools and Techniques..........................116

Smart Budget...120

Wealth Is an Illusion 125

Your Starting Point Doesn't Determine Your Outcome..130
Dealing with External Pressure.............................134
Some Money Lessons I've Learned Over the Years..136
Conclusion..140
Resources..142

INTRODUCTION

Are you tired of working all day and not seeing the results you want? Have you been working at a job that's not fulfilling yet you seem to be going nowhere near the life you want? People think that someday they'll be in a better position than they're right now but they're not committed to putting in the work it requires to get them out of the position they're in right now.

Maybe you're in buried in debt and sinking further into it everyday or maybe you've been enlightened and you're aware there's another way of living that doesn't require you to buy the mandatory new car fresh out of college and a house when you get married.

You have noticed that material items will not fulfill your needs and that it doesn't make sense to buy new stuff every single month apart from the essentials. These new items you get aren't increasing your happiness and this is confusing because it's showcased everywhere that in order to be happy you need to buy a car, house, boat and designer items.

You've realized that time is more valuable that money but money is still important because it allows you to live with the freedom you deserve to live and pursue your dreams while staying loyal to your true calling.

Your relationship with money is extremely important because even if you can earn a high income, it doesn't matter if you have no money management skills, all of it will pass through your accounts like sand through your fingers. It will end up going towards buying unfulfilling purchases such as a third motorcycle which you rarely use due to the lack of time you experience because your work demands a huge chunk of your time on a daily basis. Meaning you also end up lacking time to spend with your family and loved ones.

A minimalist budget aims to reduce the amount of places your money is going towards and to optimize it as much as possible. If it's not something you need, not helping you become a better person or be happier, then it's an expense you could possibly avoid. Streamlining is a way to erase mental clutter when it comes to budgeting. Budgeting as an activity can be fun but some people perceive it as restrictive. Instead of thinking of it as a way of restricting the money you earn, think of it as a process that's going to give you freedom by reducing your ties and obligations as well as time spent on unproductive activities.

Of course, reducing your spending isn't as fun as increasing your income, so you'll also learn the best ways I've used to start making passive income on the side while doing something you love such as **starting your own blog** for as little as $3.95 per month or talking about that which you're most passionate about.

You might notice I use many terms that are mostly seen when dealing with businesses and finance, this is because I believe that your personal finances should be managed similarly to how you'd manage a business. Think about it, if your business is not making enough revenue to cover the costs, there's something wrong that should be changed in order for it to become profitable again. The same principles must be followed when managing your personal finances and the main concepts should be learned in order to become financially literate. Sadly, most people are financially illiterate and end up spending more than they make, putting them in a dangerous situation and affecting their long term happiness.

Remember, your success or lack of success depends entirely on you. Invest in yourself, acquire knowledge and reinforce it with implementation.

The whole point of this book is to be as simple as possible so that you can easily understand all the concepts and hopefully find ways to use them in your life. If you want an advanced finance book, this is not it. I aim to teach you the basics of a healthy budget and personal finance so that you can free up your time by increasing your income while tying it with a minimalist lifestyle. Minimalism is something in which I believe deeply since it changed my life and I'm sure it can change yours as well if you give it the chance.

LIMITATION OF LIABILITY: The author does not take responsibility for the outcomes of following the advice or concepts in this book, directly or indirectly whether they result in any liability, loss or risk. I am not a financial advisor nor am I posing as one and the advice given in this book is not supposed to be taken as professional financial advice, everyone's situation is different and you should seek professional advice in order to have it tailored to your specific situation and needs. Please speak to a professional such as a financial advisor who has knowledge of your financial situation before investing or engaging in any financial activity.

You are never guaranteed to make money when you invest. You may even lose money in some cases so please do your own due diligence and speak to an attorney to understand the laws governing investing in your area, State and country.

DISCLOSURE: There are some links throughout the book, some of these are affiliate links. This means that I might get a commission if you join them and you might also get a discount or even some credit to use within the platform if you join them. Not all the links in this book are affiliates, I like to recommend the websites and services I use as I know they might be useful for you as well. Having said that, I'd never recommend something I haven't used or that I don't approve of just because it's an affiliate. What I do is I link to all the products and services which I love and then I search if they have some sort of affiliate program, not the other way around.

If you got the print version, don't worry if you can't access the links as you can get the ebook version for free as a gift for buying the print one, just make sure to download it.

BEFORE WE START

It is extremely important that you learn some basic concepts and their meanings as well as apply them as soon as possible to your situation to figure out what your starting point is.

Even though there are concepts which you will see repeated many times throughout the book, this was done with the purpose of making learning easier. Repetition will engrave concepts into your memory so that it's easier for you to learn and remember them in the long term. Therefore, next time you're faced with a situation in which the concepts can click and be useful, they'll come to you easily and fast.

Here are some of the basic concepts that are essential for you to learn:

Budget: A budget is a calculation of your income and your expenses for a period of time, usually a month.

Minimalism: Being a minimalist is searching for that sweet spot in which you have enough items to maximize your happiness but that don't restrict your lifestyle. You're totally free to do what you want and have enough time to pursue your passions, whether you work a normal job or not.

Income: This is all the money you receive per month and you can pretty much know when to expect it as it's usually paid on a set date. It doesn't matter if you earn it through your job, side job, freelancing services or investments.

Expenses: All the money you spend per month. It is usually divided by categories such as rent, utilities, food, etc.

Assets: Resources that hold value, this includes cash, investments, properties and skills or education. For the simplicity of this book, we're going to focus on those assets which are resources that generate you money.

Liabilities: Liabilities are what you owe, in other words those things which take money out of your account each month.

Savings: All of the income you didn't spend, savings are cash that you have available.

Financial Education: The knowledge and understanding of money and finance.

Financial Freedom: This is different for everyone, but for me it means not being dependent on one source of income or someone else in order to cover my expenses. In other words, you're in control of your time and money.

Financial Stability: This might also be different for everyone but it consists mostly about not worrying about your finances on a daily basis and having enough money left over at the end of the month to put towards savings. It also means you could quit your job and not have to worry too much about finding another one immediately.

As you might have noticed in the title, this book is about Minimalism applied to budgeting and finance. This is because when you're a minimalist you see an impressive change In your budget. Maybe you used to buy three items of clothes every month and have now reduced it to zero because you have enough. Or learned to value meals cooked at home a lot more and went from eating out 12 times per week to just doing it once or twice. Minimalists have an easier time with budgets because they have already realized that what matters aren't our items but the experiences and how you decide to spend your time. Being a minimalist is a great advantage when it comes to budgeting because you already know what's important in your life and which are the activities which you enjoy enough to invest in them monthly. For example if you love yoga and it makes you happy to go to the Thursday morning yoga class, there's no reason to leave it. However if you tend to skip it and it makes you anxious maybe it is time to look for another activity. The advice I can give you from this is to identify the activities that you enjoy and would like to keep in your budget as well as those ones which aren't necessary and you'd rather skip. For example, if you have a paid $20 membership you haven't used in 3 months, that would be the equivalent of throwing a $20 bill into the garbage every month. It is best to cancel it.

While minimalists tend to prefer spending money on experiences, this doesn't mean you'll go into debt just to have cool experiences, but that it is a lot more fulfilling to go on a hike and roast marshmallows than it is to buy a new shirt. That is if you like hiking and marshmallows, maybe you'd prefer to take a walk in the part and read a book or to attend a business seminar. Your preferences will affect your budget and the items or experiences you spend money on.

In the end, your budget depends on a lot of factors. Who you are and who you want to be, for example. If you enjoy traveling then there'll be a savings account for that. If you enjoy going to the movies then there'll be a designated expense for that. If you like trying out new restaurants then there'll be a higher food cost in your budget than for someone who is happy eating eggs for breakfast, peanut butter and jelly sandwiches for lunch and salad for dinner. If you're into fitness then you'll need to take into consideration the cost of protein shakes and a gym membership as well as gym clothes. In the end it depends a lot about who's doing the budget but you need to be realistic and true to yourself, so add everything you spend money on. Don't try to cheat because the only person who will end up losing is yourself.

We also need to talk a bit about minimalism itself. As you may know, minimalism is a different journey for everyone. I might be happy with just 40 items and living like a nomad while you might need to own more items and enjoy living in a nice house with a modern car. Whatever your level of minimalism or your goals, there are some basic principles to follow when it comes to managing money and expenses that minimalists seem to have engrained in them but that can be learned and applied to just this area of your life.

Mainly, to live below your means. It doesn't matter if you want to live in a tent or in a mansion as long as you can afford it, but if you can only afford a $900 rent, it's not wise to go and rent the mansion.

Happiness comes from experiences, relationships and achievements or personal development. Don't search for happiness in money because it's just not going to be there, if you're happy before having money you'll most likely continue to be happy when you acquire it. You cannot expect happiness to come along with money, happiness is something you need to develop yourself. Money is a tool which you can use for right or wrong, it is ultimately your decision. It is also an amplifier of the person you are, if you're a good person with strong values you will most likely continue this way, even if you were to become a millionaire. If you're evil, you'll just use the money you earn as a way to propagate it. Money isn't to blame for the good or evil in the world, but it will show you a person's true colors once they are in possession of it.

Minimalism will also help you reduce your monthly expenses on clothes and other items since you'll have a wardrobe that represents you and items which you'd rather not replace. You have enough and you're content with what you own, therefore there's no need to keep adding items into your space.

Throughout the book there will be an interactive section. I believe it is a lot more fun to keep you involved throughout the book and for you to share your honest answer. Hopefully, this will help you get to know yourself better and find information you weren't consciously aware of.

WHAT HAS MINIMALISM GOT TO DO WITH BUDGETING

You might find this surprising but actually, a lot. Budgets shows us where our money is going and where it's coming from. As you might expect, a minimalist will have less expenses and liabilities than a normal person because we spend less on items such as clothes or decoration. Let's take phones as an example, if you're a minimalist you understand you don't need the newest phone and on top of that, all the accessories that it includes such as 3 phone cases, a fancy phone holder for your car, a special bag to take just the phone, etc. It is enough to get the phone, one phone case and screen protector at the most.

As a new minimalist you realize that you don't need most things you currently own and that you could easily downsize your belongings to half of what they're at the moment. While people who have lived this lifestyle a little longer might have reached their optimal amount of items already.

Minimalism is living with enough items to maximize your happiness and wellbeing. While the concept of enough varies from person to person, it will most likely surprise you how little we actually need to live and be happy. Minimalism for you might mean owning only a few items while for others it might mean owning a lot more but still mindfully keeping only that which makes them happy and is useful.

Minimalism overall is about learning to be happy with less. It is about being free from the chains of objects and debt. People nowadays try to fill their emptiness with things, when in reality that's not the correct way to do so since happiness produced by the rush of buying items doesn't last. The happiness derived from physical objects fades away eventually, sometimes even a few hours after purchasing the item. You go home with your new shirts still packed in the bag and you're no longer excited about them. Buying them felt good in the moment but the initial adrenaline and endorphins that your brain released tend to fade quickly. In order to acquire some of these things, people sometimes go into debt to be able to afford them or to afford a lifestyle that's more expensive than what they earn. There's no way to justify this, as it will only lead to problems and stress in the future.

Minimalism is about not letting yourself be distracted by things, which aren't the answer to a happy life. This doesn't mean you have to get rid of everything you own, just make sure that what you keep are things which make you feel happy. Happiness comes from experiences and becoming better everyday. A better person, a better friend, a better daughter, just strive to be better than yesterday and you will end up being a fantastic person. Even if you're only 1% better than you were yesterday, you'll still experience consistent growth and massive results in the long term.

Things take a lot from you even when you don't notice it. They demand time to be cleaned and to keep them in a good state, as well as time to organize them. It takes space to keep them and money to buy them. Having things is not "free", everything comes at some sort of cost, even if it's not monetary it can take space, time, money or all of them. You need to ask yourself if this item you're about to buy is worth it.

Minimizing the amount of items you have will also free up your time. It will help you realize which things are worth keeping and giving your time to. The less items you have, the less time you need to dedicate to them. This means more time for you and the activities you enjoy and also the activities which are going to help you grow and become more productive.

If you would like to read more on the topic of minimalism itself, check out my other book: **Minimalism: How living with less makes like whole**.

Question:

What 5 activities would you do more if you had more time?

_____
_____
_____
_____
_____
_____
_____
_____
_____
_____
_____

INCOME

Income is all the money you're generating either by your own efforts or through your business or investments. You can look at it as a monthly ($2,000 per month) amount or a yearly ($24,000) amount, how you decide to measure it is up to you but we're going to be focusing on monthly income as that's where we're going to see most investments' impact. Income can come from your job, side job, side business, freelancing, rent you receive from one of your properties, dividends, passive income such as royalties or ads, and/or any other income producing activity.

So why is income so important? Aren't we minimalists after all? Well, mostly because it's what's going to cover our monthly needs as well as investments and savings. Even minimalists need money to live, although it is certainly less money than what a normal person needs, it's still needed to buy food and pay for a place to live. Plus, the more you increase your income, the more freedom you acquire and you can do with it anything you want such as help your family, travel the world, buy a house or donate more money to charity. A higher income also means you can increase your cost of living if you wished to do so although we will get to this in a few chapters. Overall, the best thing you can do is to increase your income not for the money itself but to become financially free and not have to worry about having to work at a job you don't even like just to be able to pay your bills. This will allow you to really be the owner of your time and do with it whatever it is you'd like to do. This only happens if you do it right and separate your income from your time.

Increasing your income by increasing your work load isn't such a great idea. Not only is it unsustainable but it'll also be unenjoyable. It is not the same to get an extra $1,000 per month from Youtube or a book than it is to get it by taking a half-time job on top of your other job. One of this scenarios is going to remain passive or mostly passive once you have uploaded the content while the other one will take another 5 hours or so from your day. This means you'd be working almost 13 hours per day to build someone else's dream! This is why you must find a way to separate your time from your income, there is no way to scale it if they're combined as you couldn't work 30 hours in a day even if you wanted to. It is also important to remember that most types of income pay tax, so talk to an accountant and a lawyer to make sure you're paying the correct amount of taxes each year from all of your income sources.

Minimalism is all about freeing time to enjoy the activities you love and to spend more time with your family and loved ones. Meaning that working two full time jobs just to increase your income and be able to afford expensive designer items is contrary to the philosophy. However, once you find a secondary stream of income that you enjoy you get to be less reliant on your day job and ideally you can end up moving from working a 9-5 to doing something else you actually enjoy. Now I wouldn't suggest quitting your job to become an artist if you have no plan B, it would be more sensible to stay at your job and paint in your free time until you find a way to sell your art and if it becomes a decent source of income then you can quit your job. Wrong financial decisions can take a long time to correct but if you're committed and work hard, you can change any situation you're in for the better.

Just because you're making a huge amount of money every month doesn't mean you should spend it all. You see, income is usually going to be distributed in different categories every month, for example: Part of it is going to go towards covering your expenses, another percentage is going to go towards savings, another towards investments and if you have debts then the other part will go towards repaying those debts. This would be the ideal places for your money to go. However, and you might have noticed this or are living like this, a lot of people's income usually goes directly towards covering their expenses and there's nothing left at the end of the month to save or even repay debts.

Your income is increased by your work but also your investments. You will hear me talk about increasing your income a lot throughout this book and this is because I truly believe that it can increase your quality of life. It will give you more freedom and choices to do what you want but most importantly, it'll help you help others. It is obvious that money doesn't buy happiness, and no one is saying it does, but it is a lot more enjoyable to have the choice to live how you want. Even if this means living in a van and donating your passive income to charity. In the end, it is you who decides what to do with your income.

In order to increase your income you need to increase the value you provide to the world. The market doesn't respond to needs, even if you desperately need money to pay for a health treatment, demand for your specific product or service won't increase magically and provide you with the income you think you deserve. However if you focus on solving a need in the market, people will reward your efforts with money. You don't even need to invent a new innovative way to do something, you just need to take an existing product and make it better in some way that the customer finds valuable. Find what it is that people find annoying or even hate and try to fix it. If they hate it enough to be willing to pay for it then you just found a business opportunity. Start thinking of problems and complains as opportunities to solve.

Investments will also add to your income every month. If you have an investment property that you rent for $600, then the people who are renting it are going to give you $600 every single month they're using it. If you invested money in a business when it was starting and it grew to the point in which it pays dividends then that's another stream of income for you. All the money coming from your investments will increase your income.

Your income should always be higher than your expenses. This is one of the most basic rules of having a budget but a lot of people seem to ignore it. It has always been a wise advice to live below your means. Sadly, many people go into debt to be able to afford a life they haven't earned yet, this need to have everything now has led to a massive demand for credit cards and since they don't teach us financial education in schools, most people don't know the consequences of relying on high interest debt.

Credit cards and loans count as debt, not as income. This money you're receiving to spend in whatever it is you want isn't yours and you will have to pay it back eventually and with interest. If you don't watch it, an initial $10,000 credit could turn into $25,000 over the course of a few years depending on the interest rate and how much you pay per month. Sometimes, minimum payments don't even cover the original credit amount you took out, just the interest rates which end up adding more and more money to your debt each month.

Exercise:

Write down all your streams of income, even if they generate you $0.25 per month. Everything counts and they say the first dollar is the hardest so if you have one stream which is already generating $1 then there's a great chance you can make it grow:

_____

_____

_____

_____

_____

_____

_____

_____

_____

_____

_____

Fun "fact": It is said that the average millionaire has 7 streams of income.

While I couldn't find any evidence of this to be true, I do believe they have at least 5 streams of income and most of these streams work for them instead of them having to work for the money. Think about Bill Gates or Jeff Bezos, they continuously make money even when they're eating, sleeping or just breathing. They're becoming richer just by existing. This is the leverage you can achieve by having your money work for you.

EXPENSES

Expenses are everything you spend money on. If you are going through a though time, the best idea is to reduce your expenses or increase your income. Of course, increasing your income is a lot more fun but there are situations in which the only way to be able to move forward is to decrease your expenses. At least until the rough patch is over.

Minimalism helps you reduce your expenses by focusing on acquiring and keeping only those items which bring you joy. Even though minimalism is about maximizing happiness this doesn't justify to spend more than you make. Responsibility comes first and your future self will thank you for not going into debt to fund a Mercedes even though you can only afford a used Toyota, even if the Mercedes is the "car you need to be happy". You wouldn't believe how many people I've heard talk about their cars as if happiness was derived from owning a specific car model. As you might have guessed, they're not the happiest people I know and some ended up having to sell the car because they couldn't afford the monthly payments anymore.

Your expenses are everything that you spend money on every month. Food, rent, insurance, coffee, shopping, you get me, the list could be endless. If you want to be in control of your finances you need to find out exactly where your money is going and the best and most accurate way to do this is to track your expenses. If you would prefer to track them online using an app or just by looking at your bank account statements then you will need to use your credit or debit card so that they're recorded and you receive the statement once a month in the mail or in your inbox. If you decide to use cash to make your purchases and you want to track them then you will have to keep each and every one of your receipts or have a very organized way of keeping a record of everything you buy.

Tracking my expenses was the only way I realized I was spending too much money on coffee. This is one of those purchases in which you think that $2.50 aren't going to affect you that much because it's just 2 dollars. That is until you see that you spent nearly $300 in Starbucks one month. How? Just by going in you are compelled to buy a coffee and maybe a cookie or sandwich, you haven't have lunch yet so the purchase is rationalized. This is the power of habits, you stop thinking about your actions and just repeat them daily because that's what you're used to do. If you have a habit that's costing you money then it might be time to consciously change it to something cheaper or eliminate it entirely. You could make coffee at home for 1/4 of the price and relatively the same amount of time.

What you spend money on shouldn't be calculated entirely on how much money they cost. Money isn't equal to value. How much would you pay for a glass of water right now? Probably less than $0.50 if you can just go downstairs and get water. Now imagine you're at the beach and haven't had any drinks since yesterday and a street vendor is selling bottled water. You'd probably pay $2 or even more for the same amount water. When you're about to buy something, think about if it's going to add value to your life, not just about how much it's going to cost you but if it is going to increase your happiness or skills in some way. It is not the same to spend $500 on a course that's going to help you increase your income than it is to spend it on a pair of shoes.

If you're currently working a job and make, let's say $15 per hour, you need to start thinking of expenses in a context of life hours spent rather than just money. You only have so much time and working a job that pays you $15 per hour means you have accepted each hour of your life is worth $15. So when you're going to buy a new shirt or a new pair of shoes you should approach it like: "Are these shoes worth 10 hours of my life?" rather than "$150 is a steal for these!"

Your fixed and necessary expenses such as rent and electricity can be automated so that you don't even have to think about paying them, therefore you don't have to see that money in your bank account so you don't plan how you could spend it. You can also automate payments to a savings account so that you don't have to do this consciously and think about how much money you can't use this month. The best way to manage your expenses is to have a set amount for items such as food or clothes so that you don't feel deprived but also so that you can achieve your financial goals. Whether that's high or low depends on you and on how fast you want to reach financial freedom. This goes hand in hand with the minimalist lifestyle as 1) you don't have to worry about paying everything every single month, saving you time and 2) you're saving without even noticing the money is not in your available balance, making it easier and less stressful. Nowadays there are some really cool ways to automate your savings, one of them is **Qapital**. Here you can choose to round up your payments to the nearest dollar so if you spend $2.50, it automatically rounds it up to $3 and saves $0.50 for your trip to Mexico or any other goal you're saving towards.

Don't fall into the trap of sales. As a minimalist you have another advantage here as we don't usually tend to buy stuff even if it is on sale. It can be tempting sometimes though. When you see that the price of something you want has been reduced 40% as is the case on Thanksgiving it takes a lot discipline to be able to ignore it. However you can also use these discounts in your favor. If you know that one of your favorite stores does a 40% discount on Thanksgiving and you only buy your jeans from them then you can plan your shopping so that when you do need to replace your jeans (or buy any other item you'd have bought otherwise) it matches exactly with the sale, saving you money instead of spending money you weren't planning to spend.

Beware of free stuff as they always come at a cost. When you camp outside a movie theatre for 2 days in order to be the first one to go into the cinema or when you stand in line for over an hour because someone is giving away free smoothies, you just valued your time at basically zero. If the smoothie costs $4 and you stood in line for an hour you're actually being "underpaid". What's the point of saving $4 if you're wasting the other $15 or more that your hour is supposed to be worth?

Be careful of how you spend your time and who/what you're giving your time to. Going out on dates with a million girls from Tinder might make you feel like you're the total casanova but how much time did you just waste on the app as well as on getting ready and going out? Committing to one relationship will actually make you more productive and increase your chances of becoming successful, this is if you find the correct partner. Choose carefully who you want as a partner as they could be the deciding factor to becoming successful or failing miserably.

Question:
Write down all of your expenses, including very small ones. How much did you spend last month?

_____
_____
_____
_____
_____
_____
_____
_____
_____
_____
_____
_____
_____

_____
_____
_____

Now that you have this information ask yourself: is there anyway to reduce it? Am I paying for something I'm not using? Sometimes we're subscribed and paying for memberships we're no longer using. Even if this membership is $19.99 per month, that's $240 per year that you're throwing away without noticing.

Important to remember:
Just because you greatly reduce the amount of money you're spending monthly doesn't mean you can spend it all in something else such as salsa classes. Save up as much as you can for your emergency fund, then save up until you get to a minimum of 4 months worth of expenses saved in case something happened to your primary source of income. Once you've done this you can give yourself a treat. Perhaps take that trip to Japan or Thailand you've always wanted to take. You can also save up for these goals parallel to your other savings but nothing triumphs the mental peace you get from knowing you're covered in case of emergency.

Now that you know what Income and Expenses are, try creating your current monthly budget. I suggest you do this in Excel (or Numbers) as it'll be easier to change it and compare it with your ideal budget later on.

If you have ever seen the income statement of a company, you might have noticed that it includes its income and the expenses it had to pay for during a certain period. There is also a balance sheet which includes the assets and liabilities of a company. Try thinking of your financial situation as if you were running a business. The goal is to maximize the amount of money you make, while reducing expenses (if possible) in order to increase profitability. We are now going to look at assets and liabilities, the ones in charge of your net worth.

ASSETS

Assets are one of my favorite topics to talk about as I find them to be wonderful. Think of assets as something that can hold value and be sold for a certain amount of money. Of course, these assets can also generate you money every month or every year.

The type of assets we want to focus on are the ones that are going to make you money even while you're sleeping since these are the ones that will eventually help you achieve financial freedom. This kind of assets produce income month after month without being dependent on your time to do so. Let's say you have stock photos and they make you $5 per month, this is an asset you want to build as it makes you passive income.

If you let your investments grow, you use compound interest in your favor. Compound interest is the interest you receive from reinvesting your principal sum plus what it made in interests. This type of investment usually grows rapidly and powerfully over time.

Let's say you invest $1,000 and it's going to give you a 10% return per year. In one year you would have $1,100. The original $1,000 plus the 10% interest. Now let's say that 10% return will remain the same for the next 20 years, but on the second year you already have $1,100 over which the interest is going to apply. Your initial investment of $1,000 will behave like this:

Year / Investment plus 10%

0 : $1,000
1 : $1,100
2 : $1,210
3 : $1,331
4 : $1,464.10
5 : $1,610.51
6 : $1,771.56
7 : $1,984.72 (It has almost doubled in just 7 years)
8 : $2,143.59
9 : $2,357.95
10 : $2,593.74
11 : $2,853.12
12 : $3,138.43 (It tripled in another 5)
13 : $3,452.27
14 : $3,797.50
15 : $4,177.25 (Quadrupled in another 4)
16 : $4,594.98
17 : $5,054.47 (Quintupled in another 2)
18 : $5,559.92
19 : $6,115.91 (Sextupled in another 2)
20 : $6,727.50

Compound interest is a great force you can use in your favor if you understand how it works. As you can see, in 20 years at 10% interest rate, your initial $1,000 are is now worth 6.7 times more. That's $5,727.50 more for basically just not touching it! Another thing you can notice from the example is that each time it takes less years for it to hit the next thousand, this is because the money your money is earning for you joins your initial investment to work in your favor. Even though 10% return might be a little high for most investments, you can find investments which yield 8% return on average. Returns that are around 30% are very hard to find and if someone is offering +30% yearly returns, be careful as it might not be legitimate. If it sounds too good to be true, it probably is. Research every opportunity before investing in it.

Investments will help you protect against economic forces such as inflation. Your money is worth less every year thanks to it, so even if you're not using it and you have it in a savings account or under the mattress or even in an envelope, its value will continue to decrease every year. America's inflation rate is a little bit under 3% so we will use this number to illustrate the example.

Let's say you have $10,000 in savings today. Next year, taking inflation into consideration, those $10,000 will be worth $9,700 [$10,000 - ($10,000 x 0.03)] of the spending power it has today. If you want to protect your money, you need to have it either in a savings account which gives you at least 2.5% to 3% return or in some sort of investment that gives you 3% or more per year.

This might sound scary but once you understand how the economy works you can take the necessary measures and educated financial decisions in order to protect yourself and be financially responsible.

Question:
Do you have any assets that are generating you money without you having to put in your time? What are they and how much are they generating monthly?

_____
_____
_____
_____
_____
_____
_____
_____
_____
_____

Something to think about:

I'm sure you've heard of the broken window fallacy that explains basically that destruction brings economic prosperity to everyone involved. The problem with this example is that there is one person who is actually affected by the outcome of the events, not everyone "won" in this example because he wasn't projecting that expense into his business expenses. I would like to introduce you to another example that we can see easily in our daily life. When someone creates a product or a service to add value, everyone becomes richer. Let's say you learn how to do image consultancy because it is a passion of yours and there aren't many image consultants so they're a bit expensive. You spent $1,000 on that course and plan to charge $100 per consultancy. Your initial investment would be returned within 10 consultancies, plus your investment of time depending on how much you value your time for. The person who taught you about image consultancy makes money by giving the course, and the people who hire you to give them an image consultancy get their investment back in a better personal image which might even help them get a better job or get the attention from someone they'd like to date.

Using real estate as an example, when there's land that no one is using, this land isn't worth much. Let's say you buy one of the properties and the person next to you starts building a house. Just by having a house next to your property, the value increases because it isn't just land anymore. Someone has decided to invest in the neighborhood. Now you also want to build a house and rent it because the place looks like it's going to be a nice community and it makes sense to invest. The money you spend hiring construction workers and buying materials isn't "lost", it just transforms into a house. Same with the architect you hired to do the blueprint and the engineer who's going to be in charge of the construction. The value expands to everyone involved. The workers get money for their work, the store gets money for their materials, you get a house, and if you rent it then those people get a place to live while you get compensation for providing the good.

Be careful with how the value spreads as the same happens with the opposite. Using the example of the house, if the house you built ends up being in a place that becomes dangerous or crime prone, that same house is going to lose value and it's not going to go up unless the house becomes wanted by people who are willing to pay more money for that property or if the area gets a better reputation.

LIABILITIES

Liabilities are the equivalent of a wolf in sheep's clothing. Why? Because they look nice, they sound nice, they feel nice, you enjoy them…until the moment in which the bill comes and keeps coming for 30 years until you pay it all off. What could possibly be this bad and how is it even legal? That's not even the worst part! On top of that, if you fail pay back then the bank or financial institution which gave you the loan can take the property or car away from you because it's the collateral. It's all in the small print, read it.

So what is this and how do you protect yourself from it? Well, nothing more than your house, car and anything else you financed on credit. Liabilities are what you owe, whether you owe it to the bank or your family. This means you have an obligation to pay back for them. People will try to sell you liabilities and then try to paint it as if they're going to help you and make you happier by saying things like: "This is an investment" and "Think about your future." Liabilities aren't an investment and they're not going to make you happier either. This doesn't mean you shouldn't buy a house, it just means that you should carefully plan and evaluate your budget before going into debt to finance it.

A house in which you live in is not an asset, it's a liability. Unless you're renting some part of it on **Airbnb** (if you sign up using that link you'll get $25 towards your first trip) or a something along those lines then it is a liability. Don't underestimate the power of renting you properties, you could even end up being able to live for free if your tenant pays enough rent to cover the costs of the mortgage. Other than that, it's taking money away from you every single month. Of course you have a property so all your money is actually going towards financing that property which makes a lot of people feel secure because a house is a tangible good. But what if another crisis hits and you can't afford to pay the mortgage? Guess who the real owner was all this time? Correct, the bank.

A loan is something you're borrowing, it's not yours yet until you pay for it. Same happens with cars, if you get a loan just to get the latest car and you can't afford it then you're doing something wrong. You do not have the right mindset yet. All these liabilities are costing you money. You might try to argue than your car is an asset because you "need it to make money" aka get to work but in reality it is a liability because it's not generating you any money and you have to pay to keep it. If you owned rental cars then those cars would be an asset but the car that's sitting in your garage right now is just losing value. It costs you money because it's depreciating every year you keep it, you have to repair it every once in a while as well as pay for maintenance, gas, cleaning it, etc. The good news is that you can turn your liabilities into assets by making them generate money. You have a nice car? Film a youtube video talking about all the features and show the best bits. The liability soon pays for itself and justifies the expense. You can also use it to generate a side income in your free time by joining Uber or Lyft. While this may not free up your time, it'll help you capitalize and save for future investments.

Aim to reduce liabilities or at least reduce them to something that makes sense. If you can't afford a new BMW but want a car then just get another used car from a brand that's in your price range. It is still a liability but you're not overpaying for the exact same purpose: transportation.

Question:
What are your liabilities? Do you have a mortgage payment? What about a car loan?

_____
_____
_____
_____
_____
_____

NET WORTH

Now that you have your assets and liabilities you can calculate your net worth. Your net worth is basically a calculation of how much you're worth. Properties, cars, material items, businesses and cash are going to add to it while student loans, credit card debt, mortgages and liabilities are going to rest from it.

The average American's net worth depends on the age range but the median for those who are between **35 and 44 it's $59,800**. Even if this might sound a bit worrying, the median **net worth for those under 35 is $11,100**. While this might be a little discouraging, you have the power to change your situation and end up being on the higher end of the spectrum.

Knowing how to calculate your net worth is important because it gives you a pretty good idea of where you're standing at this moment regarding your financial situation. If you don't like what you see, change your spending habits and start saving and investing more.

Question:
How much is your net worth? Calculating your net worth is a wonderful exercise and you should do it every year or so. While the easiest way to do it is on

Excel, you can take some notes in this book or add the number so that you can revisit it in the future and see how much it has changed.

_____
_____
_____
_____
_____
_____
_____
_____

CASHFLOW

Cash flow is the movement of money in a business, what goes in and what goes out. If you look at your personal finances as a business you come to the conclusion that you want a lot of money coming in and not as much coming out. What happens when more money goes out than what comes in is a scary concept: debt. Approximately 80% of Americans out of a survey of 1,000 people (available on **www.cometfi.com/details-of-debt**) are in debt (different types of debt but still debt). Being in debt isn't necessary a negative thing but it can become negative when you're using debt to finance a lifestyle you haven't earned such as buying a car or a house that's over what you can afford with your current salary or when an expense hits you unexpectedly and you have no way to cover that expense, debt comes in to save you at a high price.

The goal is to have income coming in from different sources with the force of a waterfall so that you can cover all your needs and even invest and save the extra money. Income is the money you get each month from your job or investments. So how do you increase the amount of money coming in? If you already have a full time job that means your day is mostly filled working. Please do not think getting another job will make the situation better, we've gone over this in the income chapter. The goal is to free your time, not work 12 hours per day, so you need to find another way to increase income without having to dedicate much of your time to it. At least not in the long term.

The answer is simple, increase your **passive income**. As we've seen in previous chapters, the best way to increase your income is to increase your assets since they're what generates you money without it being dependent on your time. For example if you have a property which you rent for $600 per month that's considered an asset. Summarizing, if you are living in the house then it is not considered an asset but a liability as you're paying money to live in it. Unless it has other rooms that you can rent in platforms such as **Airbnb**.

So why do you want to increase your income anyway? First, to cover all of your expenses such as rent, car, food, electricity, water, internet, etc, without worrying about making your paycheck last until the end of the month. But mostly because income that's not produced directly with your own time will lead to freedom. You need to take yourself out of the equation in order to do what you want without being restricted by a job you hate or a boss who's always telling you what you need to do. Imagine waking up (at anytime you want) and not having to face the morning traffic which robs you of an hour of your life, being able to have breakfast with your family without feeling rushed and being there watching your kids grow up.

Now just because you don't have a job doesn't mean you are the sole owner of your time. If you're a business owner you might have noticed that it feels like your own business demands a lot more time than a normal job. A business should be able to run without you micromanaging it at all times. Of course you need to set systems in place before being able to let it run by itself but you need to think of ways to automatize as much as possible from the start.

Now that you know where your money comes from and goes to and in what amounts you can start managing it correctly.

A positive cash flow means that you're spending less than what you're making, while a negative cashflow means you have to reduce your expenses since you're living above your income and probably going into debt.

In simple terms,
Positive cashflow = good, increase it
Negative cashflow = not good, turn it around

DEBT

Is debt really that bad? Well, as with anything, it depends. There are two types of debt: good debt and bad debt. Bad debt has really high interest and helps you finance liabilities, one example of this is credit card debt. Good debt helps you finance assets that are going to generate a return that pays back the debt, interest rates and gives you profit on top of that.

In general, debt isn't a good thing unless it has a very low (2%) to zero interest rate or you're going to use it to invest it in a business or another income generating source that is capable of paying off the loan plus the interest plus generate a profit. The problem is that most people who go into debt do so with a debt which has a very high interest, sometimes it is around 20%, 30% or even 40% depending on who's lending and how urgently you need the money which is downright ridiculous. You might think these are exaggerated amounts but in reality there are some credit cards that charge 30% interest per year. Why do you think banks are such a great business? If you don't believe me, go take a look at their financial statements, one of their revenue streams is going to be named "interests received from credit card debt" or something along those lines. Aren't you shocked by that amount?

Imagine paying $13,000, or even $15,000 for an initial $10,000 you got one year ago.

Now, if you remember our talk about inflation and interests a few chapters ago you will notice this is actually very similar and even related to that example.

Let's say you have a loan which charges you 1% interest per year, it is a student loan which you used to finance your Master's Degree. This loan is actually making it cheaper for you, yes you heard me right, it is making it cheaper than if you had paid for it with your money without getting a loan. Why? Just because the rate of inflation is around 3% and on top of that you have time in your favor to pay it back. This is one of those loans which has no economic incentive to pay off quickly as it actually becomes cheaper the longer you take to pay it off. In this case, the bank (or lender) is the one losing money.

Of course, debt isn't all bad news and banks can be extremely helpful when you want to start a business so now let's look at what good debt looks like. Let's say you take out a loan for $15,000 that you're going to repay in a year with 30% interest. The amount you'll have to pay (total) is going to be $19,500. However you're going to use this money to expand your business and you plan to grow your investment by 50%. If everything goes well, at the end of the year you end up with $22,500 from which you have to pay the loan plus interests, meaning you end up with $3,000 that you created from adding value and making a wise investment. Remember to take the time you invested into consideration as $3,000 might sound good for a few hours of work but if you had to work 3,000 then it's not a sensible investment.

Those are the two sides of the same debt coin, but you also need to look at the psychological side and the strain it puts on relationships and your health. Having debt, specially if you aren't able to pay it back for whatever reason, can be extremely stressful as you will have the banks or other financial institutions or individuals pressing you to pay back what you owe.

If you are in debt currently, the obvious best choice is to pay it off. Logically, the best first step would be to pay off the debt with the highest interest as this will be the one becoming more expensive each month. However there are some financial advisors who recommend to pay off the debt which is affecting you the most or that will feel like an achievement so that you're motivated to continue paying off other debts. It is different to be stalked by a bank than it is to feel tense every single time you see your family or friends. Having 3 debts to pay feels more manageable than having 5, even if those 2 debts were smaller debts with a low interest rate. Remember we are emotional beings and most of our decisions can be affected by these emotions even if we already had a logical plan in place.

If you think you can get a lower interest on your debts, call the financial institution to ask if it can be refinanced and if there's something you can work out to pay less in interests.

There are endless ways to get into debt and one of them is to not have enough money saved for an emergency. This happened to a friend of mine. What happened was that she had to pay $2,500 unexpectedly but she only had $680 in savings, which isn't that little if you consider how much the average American has in savings. You can imagine what happened next. She had to go into debt just to cover this emergency and ended up paying 20% interest on the money she got. This ended up being an extra $360 just in interests. Luckily, she was able to get the full amount (on top of her expenses) and pay it back within a year, otherwise the interests would've just continued to pile up on top of the previous ones.

Another way is when you want to finance a new phone or vacation but you don't have enough money and you *really* want to go. So you use your credit card to buy the plane ticket to Europe and 15 nights of hotel stays.

This ends up costing around $2,500 but don't worry, there's no rush to pay it back, right? Wrong! If you don't pay the full balance of your card at the end of the month you might be charged a late fee and damage your credit score. If you continue to avoid making payments, your interest rate might increase to the penalty interest rate. Don't ignore your payments, do something about this before it becomes a bigger problem. Talking to the creditors might help you in some way as this shows you're willing to cooperate, you're just in a situation in which you're not able to do so.

You can also pay off a percentage of each debt every month. Whatever method you choose, it is important that you stick to it so that you can see the results fast enough. This way you can really feel you're in the right path towards financial freedom and security.

Let me tell you a hack, if you're asking yourself "can I afford it?" you probably can't, at least not comfortably or without going into debt. Some people say the rule is that you can afford to buy something if you could buy it 5 times. If you have $1,000 in savings and you want the new iPhone, you probably can't afford it and that money would be better kept in your savings account or dedicated towards investing. However, if you have $5,000 in your savings account and you've already paid for your bills and other obligations then it makes more sense to reward yourself with the new model if it is something you really want. In the end, you're the only one who can decide how to spend your money. I'm just here to give you advice about what has worked for me on how you can spend it more wisely. Whether you take it or not is up to you and could potentially help you or not depending on how you act on the advice.

Question:
Since this is a book about budgeting, figure out exactly how much debt you have. How much do you owe, to whom and what the interest is on each one of those debts?

_____
_____
_____
_____
_____
_____
_____
_____
_____
_____
_____
_____
_____

LIFESTYLE & GOALS

"Whether you think you can, or you think you can't - you're right"
- Henry Ford

Not so long ago I interviewed a guy who didn't own a house because he loved to travel and this is the way he spent pretty much all of his life. He had recently come back from Colombia and had been in the US and Spain a few weeks ago. While this is not common, he got to achieve this lifestyle by using technology in his favor and creating passive income sources that only needed 8 hours per month to manage. In case you're curious about what he does, he owns a few small software businesses and sells products through Amazon FBA.

By figuring out exactly what you want your lifestyle to be like, you can get an estimate of how much money you need to make per month and what you can do to achieve this. Therefore, it is directly related to your goals.

There are a lot of questions you need to ask yourself about money and the answer depends on where you want to end up and who you want to be. If you want an early retirement, let's say when you're 35, then you need to start working on it as early as possible as well as investing to multiply your money since saving alone probably won't get you there fast enough. Needless to say, I don't think he'll ever go back to working at a job unless it's at one of his many companies. Now that you have an idea of your desired lifestyle, you need to make an action plan of how you're going to get there.

Big goals generate action. You need to make your goals big enough so that they keep you motivated. You need a reason why to stick to your budget and work towards your dreams and if it's not big or powerful enough then you'll most likely fail as there's no downside to spending all your income on items which will give you instant gratification rather than an amazing future.

Your goals should be specific, measurable and have a time frame in which you intend to achieve them. It is different to want to make an extra $100 by the end of the week than in two years. If you don't give yourself a deadline you'll probably keep postponing the necessary actions you need to take in order to reach your goals because you think you have plenty of time. Newsflash: you don't, so start putting in the work today. Your goals should be measurable because you need a way to measure your progress and how close or far away you're from your goal. This also allows you to come up with a strategy which will provide you with the daily and weekly necessary steps to take in order to reach your goal.

Divide your goals into the specific areas of your life which you want to target.
Since this is a financial book we are going to focus on the financial aspect but you can use these goal setting techniques for other areas as well.
These areas could be:
Finance/money: I make _____ per month as passive income by _____
Self-development:

_____
_____

Health:

_____
_____

Family:

_____
_____

Friends:

_____
_____

Spirituality:

_____
_____

I understand each person has a different goal (or goals) in each one of the different areas so there is a blank space for you to write down your goals. Make them big enough so that they motivate you, don't be afraid to dream big.

If you believe you can achieve something then you will find a way to do so. If you believe you can't then your subconscious will find a way to sabotage yourself because then you're right and we love being right. The moment in which we fail we tend to justify it with petty excuses such as "I knew I wasn't going to get that raise, I'm too ____" Don't do this. You are smart and capable enough for that raise, keep working towards it.

Question:
What are your goals for this year? Divide them by area and write them in a way that makes them specific, measurable and give you a time frame to achieve it. Don't worry if you don't reach them in that time as you can always keep aiming towards them. What's important is to become better everyday. You can write only your financial goals or include your other goals as well.

_____
_____
_____
_____

_____

_____

_____

_____

_____

_____

_____

Trying to figure out what you want to do in the future can be a bit stressful, but it's going to help you in the long term. My goals changed a lot when I realized that I wasn't aiming towards the big house and new car that everyone sets as destination but towards freedom. Minimalism helps you reach a level of freedom hard to attain by other means and I didn't want to sacrifice my freedom for more income, so I had to find a way to fit my minimalist lifestyle choice and my financial goals.

Minimalism and income impact lifestyle at an unbelievable level, for me the most notable differences were evident in my attitude towards life, the way I traveled and how I spent my time. I started writing down one thing for which I was grateful every single day, this helped me notice that I was surrounded by abundance. I learned how to travel lightly as it is all about the experience, not about what you bring. Lastly, I learned how to value my time. I stopped wasting hours every day on social media and switched it towards reading business books, becoming more productive and working towards my dreams instead of liking motivational posts.

MINDSET & HABITS

> "Whatever the mind of a man can conceive and believe, it can achieve"
> - Napoleon Hill

If I told you there is one thing, one single thing which can tell me whether you will be successful or unsuccessful in any area of your life, would you believe me? Well, you can pretty much predict how someone's life is going to look like in about six months by looking at what they're doing now. Your future depends almost exclusively on your habits. It is what we do every single day that determines where we're going to be.

If you are overweight and change your habits to those of a healthy person, you will eventually become that person and reach a healthy weight. If you commit yourself to exercising 5 times per week and eating healthy then it is just a matter of time until you achieve the goal you set for yourself. The same happens with productivity and good money habits.

Question is, how long can you last? The whole point of developing a good habit is to continue doing it. You also need to work on eliminating those bad habits you're used to living with. There are habits which can harm you and that are extremely difficult to get rid of, one example of this is the habit of smoking. Many people try to quit and fail miserably because it's not that easy and it requires a level of commitment that many people lack. So they go back to what's easy which is to continue smoking, even when they know that this is going to hurt them in the future. Build habits that make you a better person so that you don't have to change harmful habits when it's too late.

Habits are what make you successful. There is no such thing like an overnight success, that overnight success took years in the making. Just because you only see the moment in which they reach the top doesn't mean they didn't spend hundreds of hours preparing, planning and training. You can't see the sleepless nights they had to go through because they had to finish lifting, practicing, programming or editing. Even Youtubers put a lot of time and effort into their videos. They have to come up with an idea of what to film, make some sort of draft about what they're going to talk about, film the video (sometimes many times because they stutter or mispronounce a word), edit the content (which includes reviewing all of the material and keeping only the snippets which they consider are going to be either useful or entertaining to their audience), find music that's free to use and add it to their videos, write the description, come up with an attractive title so that people click on it, etc, etc. That 10 minute video that you just watched took 2 hours to make. Not so simple being a Youtuber now, huh? And they probably spend at least another two hours going through the comments on both the video and on social media and replying to as many as they can because it is important to engage with the audience.

The first comment I usually get when I tell people I'm a writer is "Woah, I could never write a book." and you know what the saddest part is? They're probably right. If you set barriers to what you can achieve then you will never achieve it because you'd have to go through all the mental hurdles you placed before you even start trying. The only reason I'm able to write and finish a book is because I am committed to doing so. Yes, it is my passion but just because it is something I enjoy doing is not like I just stare into my computer screen and type whatever comes to my mind and then publish whatever mess came out. It takes planning and consistency to be able to write a book, let alone finish it.

One day, a guy asked me where I found the inspiration to write. I simply replied that I believe discipline precedes inspiration. I write when I'm inspired and when I'm not inspired because I made writing everyday a habit. Habits go hand in hand with your mindset as this is what's going to dictate your reality. If you want to change your results, you need to change your mindset. There is no way you can just sit on your couch without doing anything and expect to become rich in the next year. Let alone watching TV. You need to change this habit for something more productive such as reading, in order to make this transition without giving into resistance, you need a bigger reason. This is where your mindset will save you from harmful or wasteful habits, having a growth mindset will prevent you from spending all your time in front of the TV and will make you spend your time in activities that are going to benefit you in the future.

Another example instead of the TV is the time we spend in our car. Most people use it to listen to music without realizing that they could be educating themselves on any topic they'd like. Time we spent in traffic is indeed wasted time, but that doesn't mean we can't make the most out of it by listening to audiobooks on business, sales, nutrition, marketing, economics, architecture, etc. After all, education needs to continue when we graduate in order to keep improving everyday. I usually listen to books on **Audible** or videos on Youtube about a particular topic I want to educate myself in or when I want to motivate myself.

I've noticed that one of the reasons why people end up not succeeding is because they didn't think failure was an option, they just hoped everything was going to turn out for the best without making a conscious effort to change but they ended up being in the same position at 60 than when they were 35. If you ask any 35 year old person how they think their life is going to be when they're 60, they're probably going to tell you they're in a totally different position, living in a better place with a better car, probably about to retire as they're optimistic. The reality is a lot harsher than that. Most Americans can't afford to retire because they either have no savings or the savings they have on their retirement accounts are worth a lot less than what they'd need to retire. We are talking about 70+ year old people here, do you think this is the answer they would have given you at 30?

Uncertainty and an aging population are shifting the system we are used to. Luckily, we're in an era in which you can become a lot richer a lot faster if you learn how to leverage the tools around you. Once you realize you might have to go through a rough 2 - 5 years in order to live the future almost nobody gets to enjoy then you start the path towards financial freedom. It might be long and it will definitely be challenging but it will be worth it. You're going to trade 2 years of hard work and dedication for a lifetime of freedom. Living the life nobody wants to endure in order to live the life no-one can afford to live.

Let me tell you one thing, I used to be a lazy couch potato. I talked a lot about becoming a millionaire and where I wanted to be and who I wanted to become but my actions seemed to indicate the opposite. I used to spend a lot of money on disposable items such as clothes, food and makeup instead of investing it in myself and my education. It hit me hard when I realized I was in exactly the same position I used to be 2 years before. How could that be? I've been working towards becoming a millionaire, right? That's if you count spending 4 hours per day liking motivational quotes on Instagram and binge watching Netflix series. Then I decided to cut out my old habits entirely, I deleted both Instagram and Netflix from my phone, along with Candy Crush, Facebook, Pinterest and every other app I wasted too much time in.

With all this new found time I decided to work on something and so I started writing books, started a blog and on the side I was making Youtube videos, trying to find out an activity that was going to make me a decent amount of money monthly. These three business models are amazing income generators but they weren't working for me. Nothing really changed because I was spending my time in many different activities but not really committing to one in particular. This period didn't generate much income but man, it gave me a ton of valuable skills. I learned how to design and build websites, do the whole production process of a video from planning to filming to editing and publishing and I also taught myself discipline and self motivation by writing books (not as easy as it seems but doable).

One question I ask myself now before I start any activity or business project is:
Am I committed to dedicating 2 years of my life to this? And if the answer is no then I do not pursue it. The problem with people is that they want everything immediately, they want money now without putting in the effort. The problem with this is that money is an effect of value created but they expect to skip that part. It takes the average business around 2 years to reach break-even point. If you're not willing to give your project at least 2 years then you're not going to be there to reap the rewards from growing your business. Once you're past breakeven point then that's when you start seeing profit if the business is doing well.

You need to keep your limiting beliefs in check because they will come bite you. If you were raised in a society which actually punishes people who acquire wealth then you have even more limiting beliefs that are holding you back. Believing rich people are evil will prevent you to become rich because you don't want to become evil. See where I'm going with this?

Why do you believe money bad? There is no logical reason with which you can support that statement. If the person who became rich suddenly became a bad person it's because they weren't a good person to start with. Money works as a multiplying factor, if you are good then with money you will be able to do great things and help thousands of people but if you're a bad person before acquiring the money then you will just become worse and do more evil. It depends on what you want to do and how you want to be remembered.

Another way in which money is a multiplying factor is when you want to start a business, it's not the same to start with whatever is in your bank account than to start with a handsome budget that you can invest in R&D, IT, marketing and sales departments.

Also, who told you money is scarce? Maybe you just haven't found a way to acquire it yet. If you traded in the stock market you could get $1,100 in about 3 seconds. Of course you need training for this but it's doable. Apple's market cap is $1 trillion. If that's not proof that there is indeed money out there, I don't know what is. Problem is, someone else has it, and it is your money. You deserve to be wealthy and to enjoy life without worrying about money every month.

It is a lot more fun to live in abundance and you can do much more good by doing so.

If you have nothing left to lose then what are you waiting for? If your starting point is rock bottom then there's only one way to go and that way is up.

Question:

What are some limiting beliefs that you have? These can be either about yourself or about money. Identify them so that you can start working on correcting them.

_____
_____
_____
_____
_____
_____
_____
_____
_____
_____
_____
_____

I know one of the hardest parts about starting your journey to financial freedom is to believe in yourself. I was lucky enough to be surrounded by supportive people and have one mentor who constantly motivated me just by his confidence in that I was going to become successful. You might be luckier and have even more people in your support system, or not as lucky and be surrounded by loved ones who seem to demotivate you.

Whatever your situation is, I want to tell you that I fully believe in you.

I believe that you can achieve everything that you want and more. You have all that's necessary to become successful and achieve all of your goals to make your dreams come true.

Even if you don't believe in yourself yet, I believe in you. If you were waiting for a sign to take the first step towards the life of your dreams, this is it.

You are completely in control of your life.

HOW TO INCREASE YOUR INCOME

We've talked about this in a previous chapter but I wanted to give it more attention as I truly believe having more money will help you live a better life. Whether you want to spend your money on vacations, a nicer house, investments or education, money gives you the freedom to do so without having to worry about how you're going to afford it.

Value
First you need to find a product or service which people need and are willing to pay for. It could be anything that's on demand and preferably with no low or no competition as it will be easier for you to position yourself that way. If you enter a market that's highly competitive then customers have no reason to buy your product unless it is highly differentiated in some way that's attractive to them. You don't need to invent anything new, just find one aspect of a product or service that could improve.

Reach
How many people are you able to reach with the business or job you're in right now?
Let's take KDP as an example, when I publish a book on **Amazon** then it has the possibility to reach any person

who uses Amazon, speaks English and is searching for a book on this topic.

The same goes for a blog or a social media account, you pretty much have worldwide reach without the logistics of having to expand there as if you had a physical franchise such as Subway, which you can still find in pretty much every corner of the world. You need to find a way to sell your products to more people and you can only do this by reaching more people. You can do this with the help of the internet and sell online with the help of a distributor or even **Amazon FBA**.

Market Research

It's no fun to come up with a product, develop it, do the whole marketing and sales strategy, invest in R&D, manufacture the product and then not sell a single unit when you launch.

This can and should be avoided at all costs.

Failing fast is the best thing that can happen to you as it is a lot cheaper to fix a mistake in the starting stages than it is to fix it the day of the launch. This will not only save you money but also time, resources and workforce expenses.

Marketing

It doesn't matter if you have the best product ever created if no one ever hears of it and the company dies within months because you failed to get customers.

One of my favorite phrases I've heard in the past year is by one of the founders of **Airbnb** in which he said that they kept launching because if you launch and no one notices you can continue to launch again and again until something happens. A launch is a great way to increase the number of people who will be using your product or platform.

You also need to remember that some things take time and it's very likely that you won't start with a huge income right away. Coca-Cola started selling only 9 servings per day on average on its first year. Want to guess how much they sale nowadays?

When it comes to marketing you need to be creative in order to find a way to make your customers think about you frequently.

There's also a huge power in advertising during a high sales period such as Black Friday or Cyber Monday and during the Amazon Prime day. Even if you aren't aware this is going on as a seller, you will experience a peak on your sales because of the amount of traffic on Amazon during those dates. Imagine if you had anticipated the effect and set systems in place to catch the wave. Start thinking as a producer rather than a consumer and you will find endless ways to make money.

I'm always fascinated by how brands like Apple pretty much release a product and people sell it to themselves (guilty as charged). Once you see the new iPhone there's just something inside you that yells it is a necessity and finds ways to get it. This often justifies going into debt just to acquire a new phone, which isn't a very smart decision financially. What I'm trying to illustrate with this point is that you should also aim to create loyal followers such as Apple's.

Growth

My dad always tells me to remember that even elephants start small. I remember being very frustrated a few years ago because I had a business which wasn't generating as much as I wanted it to and I felt I was working in it for hours every single day. One day I realized that the business itself was growing at a massive rate for any business, at almost 150% every single month but I hadn't realized because the initial growth was so small it was barely noticeable. It wasn't until the second year that it grew so much it actually became sustainable and started generating more than I could've imagined. If you compare it to the elephant saying, you'll realize it actually makes sense.

Elephant pregnancies last for almost two years, which are two years in which you can't even see the baby elephant but it is there and it is growing and becoming bigger and bigger each month. It starts with a tiny embryo which is so small it's basically undetectable. And even when elephants are born they're still tiny compared to adult elephants which can end up weighting up to 6,300 kg. Taking into consideration they're born weighting around 100 kilograms, they're already heavier than most adult humans but they're still 1.5% the size of an adult male elephant. The point is, even if you can't see results right now but you're putting in the necessary effort consistently, you will eventually get there. Just because you're starting from nothing doesn't mean you can't grow to an incredible size and become a mighty and powerful elephant.

Find a way to generate a second or even third stream of income. The best income you can find is passive income since it doesn't depend on your time to earn you money. You literally earn money while you sleep and since it operates in worldwide markets it has a massive reach, even people in China, India, Europe or Hawaii could be reading the blog post you posted earlier that day and earning you income in Ad revenue or affiliates.

Replicability & Scalability
If you start a business which can be easily replicated you basically have a blueprint that can and will probably work for other people, in other countries or cities and for other businesses as long as the necessary tweaks are made.

It needs to be scalable so that you can grow with the demand and not fall short when your clients want more of what you're offering.

Now that you have some concepts of what's preferable, here are some ways you can generate income by leveraging the power of the internet, not all of them are completely passive and you do have to make an upfront investment of time, money or both in order to set this new source of income but it is completely worth it.

Imagine this: you are successful at saving money and end up saving $10,000 in one year on top of your emergency fund and your other fund to survive 6 months without working... Now what? Savings by themselves aren't going to do much for you apart from devaluate, even if you have them in the bank as the interest rates are usually lower than inflation.

The answer is to invest, make your money work for you to generate more money. This is how you build your assets. The type of investment you decide to start with depends on a few factors.

The amount of money you have
It is different to start investing $10,000 than it is to invest $1,000, $100 or even $100,000. The more

money you have, the more options you get. If you want to start sooner, you will probably start with less capital but don't worry, thanks to the internet we no longer need a high capital to start building a profitable business or to start investing.

The industries you're familiar with
Would you let your grandma be in control of your cryptocurrency investments? Probably not because she doesn't know much about cryptocurrencies or even the internet. Unless she's a pretty cool grandma and even knows about how blockchain works. Anyways, back to the point: it's the same with you so why are you thinking about investing in something you have no knowledge on. The best idea would be to learn about cryptocurrency or seek the help of someone who knows about it and is doing well before investing your money on it.

Risk tolerance
It is different to invest in a business which promises you 20% growth in one year than to lend it to a company which offers 6% but you're certain you'll get your money back. Let's say you're going to invest in a startup that looks promising. This could go one of two ways: awesome or horrible. All of your investment could be lost due to one error or mistake, however if it does well it could even become a unicorn (this is highly unlikely)

or generate a nice return. If you're going to lose all your hair due to the stress of having a high-risk investment then it is a lot healthier for you to stick to safe investments. Also, if someone is offering something that sounds "too good to be true," it probably is, so do your research before you invest in anything.

Acquiring assets is a way of transforming money into tangible sources of income which have intrinsic value. Think about money for a second, the value it has is pretty much the value we assign to it. Years ago, the dollar and the pound were backed by gold but not anymore. Nowadays currencies are backed by supply and demand, basically controlled by the government. This means that if the government decides to print double the money that's in circulation at the moment, the value of the currency will go down relative to the amount of dollars in circulation. If the money mass was $1 trillion and they print another $1 trillion, the new money mass will be $2 trillion but it will hold its original $1 trillion value, meaning now you need $2 to buy something which was worth $1. There was no value "created", just devaluation of the currency. Of course this is an oversimplification of the situation and there are a lot more factors to take into consideration but as a citizen you have the power to decide if you want to accept the money or not as payment. However, having a standard way of exchange is essential to facilitating financial interactions between individuals or entities. Before I go deeper into economics, I'll just simplify by saying that while gold keeps its value because it's, well…gold, currencies fluctuate and the best way to catch that value that they have right now is to start investing. Invest to turn intangible value into intrinsic value.

The assets you acquire or businesses you build are meant to give you a return on your investment. The advantage of being able to use the internet is that you can start with really low capital, here are some examples of side income sources you can start:

BLOGGING
Blogging is a great way to write about a topic that you're passionate about and being paid for it. It is true that since barriers of entry are very low for this type of business that it has become saturated, however if you upload quality content that people are searching for and find useful then your blog will become successful. You cannot rely on just uploading anything and then hoping to get massive traffic and get paid by Google Adsense. You need to differentiate yourself from all the other blogs that are out there if you want to own a profitable blog.

Starting a blog isn't as expensive as starting other side businesses, the cost of buying a domain for a year is around $20 and the hosting is usually around $100 per year. However, you can **start your own blog for as low as $3.95 per month and with a free domain** by starting your blog with **Bluehost** and through my link. **Bluehost** is very friendly to use as a first time user and starting your first blog is super simple to do.

If you want to keep costs low you can write your own articles but if you prefer a passive income source you can use resources such as **Fiverr** or Upwork to hire freelancers who can write articles for you.

For royalty free images you can use a fantastic site called **Unsplash** to download high quality pictures which you can use for pretty much everything (read their terms and conditions first). This is the one I use and I have found that they have a library big enough for you to find pretty much anything that you'd want. Of course if you want something more specific you might want to try one of the paid stock image sites as they have more variety and a bigger portfolio.

YOUTUBE

Youtube is an amazing option because you can start with stuff you have right now, with less than $25. You could even start with $0 if you wanted. There are really no excuses as to why you couldn't start with youtube because it is very simple. Some of the items you might need are:

- Your own phone to film.
- Tripods that are $12 on Amazon
- Designing a thumbnail will take you like 10 minutes or you can order one for $5 from **Fiverr**
- Most computers have a video editing software or you can download a paid one if you're looking for a more professional option.
- Uploading your content to Youtube is free.

If you look at the statistics of how many hours of video are uploaded per minute to Youtube (around 400) you would probably think that this is oversaturated and it doesn't make sense to even try it. But when you look at it from the consumer's standpoint and behavior you will realize that people still consume a lot more videos than what is uploaded. Even if you're a Youtuber yourself you will still watch someone else's videos every once in a while. If you watch 5 videos per week and then upload 1 or 2 then there's still a gap between supply and demand that you're not filling but someone else might. There's also the videos that were already available on the platform from previous years, but some of these lose relevance and receive less views as time goes by.

Depending on the type of videos you want to upload and the type of channel you want to have, it will take you between 10 minutes and 3 hours just to produce one video, so this is something to take into consideration if you think being a youtube consists only on recording a low quality video and uploading it as it is to the platform.

Once again, since this book is about minimalism, there is a way to take yourself out of the equation as much as possible and delegate it to someone else. You can actually hire people to edit your videos and write your video descriptions for you. Of course this comes at an extra cost but it will free up your time so that you can do the most important activities such as filming.

I would strongly suggest you start (specially if you have a limited budget) doing as much as you can yourself. This way you will learn how everything is done so that you can be aware of how much work it is and how to do it in case you have to edit your own videos and also save a few dollars to start as lean as possible, at least until you have enough capital to invest in making this a passive income source.

AMAZON KDP

This is the Amazon branch in which you can publish your own books, you can either write them yourself or hire a ghost writer to write them for you. You can create your account for free but you will need to know how to write, proofread, edit, format and upload your books or have enough capital to hire someone from **Fiverr** or **Upwork** to do it for you.

The amazing part about this business model is that you only need your computer and internet access to start with it. Let's say you have your book ready for publishing, you just go into the **Amazon KDP website**, create your account, publish the book and start seeing the sales rolling in. Of course it is a bit more complicated than that and you need to know enough about marketing to make sure your book sells because it doesn't make sense to invest time and money into a book that's only going to sell 2 copies.

I love Amazon by the fact that it gave writers an opportunity to reach more audience without having to go through a system that required them to pay thousands of dollars just to start and then give up a huge part of the royalties for the books sold. It was slow and it wasn't working fast enough to fulfill the high demand of authors wanting to publish their books. When you publish on Amazon, the demand itself (customer) decides which books are worth it and rates them accordingly to how much value they added and if they're written correctly. If you sell a lot of books but also get a lot of returns, the content of the book wasn't good enough for the customers to believe it was worth the price. Although you did everything else well enough to acquire a new customer, you couldn't manage to keep him or her.

Some points to take into consideration if you want to start publishing on KDP:

- Be realistic, we all judge books by their covers, so you do need to invest in a decent cover. This is the only expense I'd recommend you to spend money on.
- Check if there's a demand for the book you plan to publish before writing it. You can have the best book ever, but if no one is looking to buy it then it'll go unnoticed.
- Make sure there are no writing mistakes and that the book is easy to read and understand.
- Choose the correct keywords.

If you would like to learn more about kindle publishing, there are a ton of videos on Youtube on this topic that you can watch and learn from.

AMAZON FBA

This platform lets you sell products on Amazon. Doing market research will force you to switch your mindset from a consumer's to a producer's. What do people want? Make sure to conduct appropriate market research before launching your first product. Is there actually a need in the market for this? Or are you trying to fulfill a selfish desire to only sell what you love?

You can outsource your items from China, there is this awesome Website called **Alibaba** in which you can talk to suppliers in China to outsource pretty much anything you could think about. Just make sure to contact different providers as well as get samples for the products you want to sell. It's not the same to look at a picture than to see and feel the product in person. Some of these products can smell weird or have other qualities which your client might dislike and never buy from you again. This is why it is so important to only sell something that you would use or that you consider the quality is high enough to actually sell it. A shitty product will lead to one star reviews and eventually decrease your sales until no units are being bought. While a quality product with high demand and good reviews will continue to sell for an extended period of time. Focus on the long term, don't fall into the trap of making money fast at whatever cost, it is a lot more profitable to build a brand.

Once again, there are plenty of Youtube videos which you can watch that teach you everything you need to learn before starting. If you don't consider this to be enough, there are also plenty of courses which you can invest in to make sure you have proper guidance.

INSTAGRAM

Having a decent sized following on a social media platform could mean an extra source of income for you if you know how to use its potential. Just look at Kylie Jenner, whether you like her or not, it is undeniable that Kylie is an extremely smart business woman. She found a way to sell a new makeup product to her millions of followers, granting her the billionaire status.

That's something to admire. Launching a makeup brand for you might be out of the question at the moment but there are other ways in which you can earn money with your social media accounts.

Sponsored posts: some brands reach out to you when you have a big audience that's active and engaged. You can be paid for your posts if you have an audience of 10,000 followers or more. If you're in the fitness niche, you might have brands approach you with exercise clothes or protein powders for you to try out or even to sponsor one of your posts. Kim Kardashian has been paid up to $500,000 per sponsored post. While I'm aware I'm not Kim Kardashian and you're probably not Kim either, you can still get paid $1,000 per post if you have a niche audience that brands are interested in.

Shoutouts: Believe it or not, some people pay other accounts to get a shoutout and hopefully acquire more followers. You could be charging around $300 for a shoutout if you have a following of 100,000 people. You might be able to charge more or less depending on your industry but the good thing is that you are able to negotiate how much you want to charge until you find an amount that's convenient for you and the person who wants the shoutout.

Giveaways: This is an easy strategy that can help you get followers and it is to set up a giveaway. I've noticed travel blogs sometimes offer a trip or a two night stay at a hotel to their followers and other people in the platform if they follow them, it usually goes along the lines of: "like this post and tag 3 friends". This is a great way to reward your followers but you need to be careful as it could dilute your loyal audience with people who are only in for the prize. It's also less expensive than paying for a sponsored post in someone else's profile.

Affiliate marketing: If you're an affiliate for a product or service then you can promote it in your profile by uploading pictures and content. If you connect the customer with the seller you receive a commission.

Promoting your own products: You can also create and promote your own products on your social media such as your blog or a course you created. It is very important that you do not buy your likes and followers because if they're not real or interested in what you're offering then it will be of low or no use to the brands wanting to work with you and this is something they'll notice after the first partnership ends and probably will never want to work with you again. Be legit.

AFFILIATE MARKETING

This is when you love a brand or product and you decide to talk about it to your audience in order to sell it. You will receive a commission each time there's a sale and it is a win-win situation for everyone involved. The producer sells their product, the customer is presented with a product that's useful for him or her and you receive a commission.

Make sure everything you're marketing is a high quality product which you know that your followers or readers are going to enjoy or find useful. If you damage your credibility you could damage an important relationship with your followers, who are the ones that help your business stay alive.

It has to be coherent, you can't be talking about how you take care of your hair and then introduce a product on how to start a blog. It confuses everyone and they're probably not watching the hair tutorial because they want a blog, they just want shiny hair. Help them get shiny hair! A product that would make sense in that scenario is one that keeps your hair shiny all day and is made from all natural and organic ingredients, be creative and coherent.

If you would like to take an **awesome course on affiliate marketing**, this is the one I recommend and it is by Michelle Schroeder-Gardner, the founder of **makingsenseofcents.com**

DROP SHIPPING

One of the best ways to make money and reducing your collateral is to do drop shipping. This is when you find an item that's selling for $10 in a marketplace such as aliexpress and post it on another site such as Shopify for $20. If someone clicks on your product and buys it, then you can go and buy it and have it delivered to the person's address. The best part about this is that you don't have to have inventory, you can just order the product when there has been a sale and the company you order it from will package it and ship it to your customer.

STOCK PHOTOS

It is as easy as taking a high quality picture and uploading it to one of the many stock image sites. I personally use **Shutterstock** because I have found it to be the easiest one to use but there are many others that you can use as well. These sites usually pay you a royalty when someone downloads your picture to use it for a blog post or another activity. A high quality image can end up making you $100 per month if you know what type of stock pictures people want.

In order to help your photos be more profitable you need to make them easy to find. Make sure to choose the right name, description, keywords and tags. If I want to find a picture of a banana, I will type in the word banana so if your picture of a banana is under "tropical tree with beautiful yellow fruits" there is a very small chance I'll come across it.

ONLINE COURSES

Online courses are one of the best ways in which you can start earning a passive and significant income online. It only requires that you have an ability which others would like to learn, examples of this are coding, website design, fashion consultancy, monetizing a website, financial knowledge, etc. You will need an audience in order to have a successful product launch but you can leverage other people's audiences by reaching out to public figures in your niche. Always make sure that you're offering valuable information and to keep your customer happy.

One way of finding people to help you promote your content is to look for similar profiles on instagram or youtube or searching what you want to promote online and finding blogs that are aligned with what you plan to teach.

If you want to take an awesome course on Online Courses and making money online, there's **this one** by Mariah Coz from **Femtrepreneur**.

FACEBOOK GROUPS

There are some very successful facebook groups which charge you a monthly subscription. If you build a community who is interested in a certain niche then a facebook group could be the best way to monetize it and add value to everyone. This might require you to be active on facebook and interact with the members of the group on a daily basis. Remember they're your customers and it is a lot cheaper to keep a customer happy and recurring than it is to acquire more customers.

This particular option doesn't fall into the category of passive unless you find someone to help you manage the group and answer questions. I personally use and love Facebook groups because they're filled with people on the same journey as me and we can all learn from each other.

FREELANCING

Not passive either but you can work from anywhere in the world and during your own hours you set yourself. If you want to work from 2 a.m. to 8 a.m. then you're free to do so, just as if you want to work from Starbucks, your bed or the beach.

The only problem with this model is that it is still dependent on your time for you to generate income, so if you stop working you will stop receiving payments.

One of the many positives is that you get paid directly to your bank account every month and you can usually charge before getting to work which is awesome because many people who offer their professional services charge afterwards and it can take a long time to get paid and some don't even get paid.

Some cool websites to offer your freelancing services are **Fiverr** and **Upwork**. You might want to start offering a cheaper service than the competition so that you can get enough positive reviews and then increase your price.

STOCK MARKET

Whether it is by day trading or buying and holding stocks for the long term, the stock market has been vehicle that has made a lot of people superrich. As with anything, there's also the other side who thinks it is a scam because they lost $1,000 in two days. Be careful, as with any investment there are a lot of risks involved when trading and you need to have a solid strategy if you want to start day trading. To trade, you need to have a plan based on logic and be strong enough to resist emotional urges to sell or buy. The stock market will recognize and take all the money away from those unexperienced individuals who are not familiar with it and let their trades be managed by emotions rather than by market analysis and education.

If you're not willing to put in the work to learn how the stock market behaves, this may not be for you.

There's also an error percentage so even if you have the best trading strategy out there, you might still lose money some days and even months. If you manage to have 80% accuracy that's considered high and making 10% on your capital everyday is possible but you'll need to have a solid strategy for trading.

There are optimal times to trade and the best is to look for high volume as this is where you'll make the most money.

If you're in for the long term, buy stocks from those companies which you love and use. Owning a stock is like owning part of this company, you wouldn't want to own a company that sucks. Stick with what you know is a good brand. If you'd like a good example of who to follow when it comes to buying and holding stocks, research Warren Buffet.

If you'd like to start investing in stocks, the sites I've seen most people love and recommend are **TD Ameritrade** and **Robinhood**. These sites are for Americans or people who live in the U.S.

However, if you're outside the U.S. you can use **IQ Option**, this is the site I use personally and that my friends who trade use as well. Do your research to make sure that you can legally use each one of the trading platforms as most have area restrictions.

How to receive your payments

In most cases you just link your bank account to the sites and they will deposit the money directly when you have reached the minimum amount stated in their website.

However if you live outside the US in a country to which they don't make direct deposits to, you can create an online bank account with **Payoneer**. This is extremely useful if you live in a place such as Latin America in which it would take a bit longer to receive a check from them and then it would be more expensive because of the fees of the international transfers between banks. By using **this link**, they will give you and me both $25 if you sign up.

No excuses:

If you want a fantastic body, you need to train and eat healthy. There's no way around it. The same happens with finances, if you want a healthy bank account and cushy savings then you need to be aware of how your money is flowing when you get it.

Get a mentor

Nowadays you don't even need to live in the same city as your mentor. You have the advantage of the Internet, and even if you don't have direct access to the mentor you want you can still watch their interviews and videos on YouTube or save up until you can attend one of their seminars or even schedule a coaching call with them.

SHOULD I GET A JOB OR START A BUSINESS?

This is something I asked myself for years when I was in a position in which I had no defined road to follow. I was lost and didn't have anyone to talk to about this. The conclusion I got to is that it depends entirely on you. I also figured out is that it depends on your risk tolerance as well as your goals.

If you're stressed because you can't pay your bills on time every month, imagine how stressed you're going to be when you have to ask for another loan because you miscalculated cash flow.

However you also need to think about what would happen if you lost your job today.
There's risk in every investment, and in this case what you're investing is your time. Time is one of the few things you can never get back or more of.

The safest way to do it is to start a side hustle while you're working or to use your income from work to invest it in your new business. This way you won't be letting go of one branch until you've taken hold of the next one.

Get a job that fulfills a need in the market. Even if you get a degree it isn't a guarantee you will succeed or even get a job. The job market is becoming more difficult each year due to an excessive supply of people with college degrees and a lack of new jobs. This is a simple matter of supply and demand. If there's too much supply of something then the value of that good is going to decrease because it's so common and there is more competition. If there are 50,000 individuals with MBAs in a town but the town only needs 2,000 then there's no way those 50,000 will be employed in the job they want and will most likely start moving towards other jobs and other industries or even other places. There's a high chance a few of them will end up working at McDonald's or Starbucks. Not that there's anything wrong with working at any of these establishments but these specific people would be overqualified for the job and underpaid for their abilities. Fun fact about me: they actually turned down my application to work at Starbucks. I was rejected from a job that paid $2 per hour when I was 18. This is in part why I became an entrepreneur, nobody was hiring.

You also need to consider than having a job and having a business are fundamentally different in a lot of aspects. In one scenario, you have no control but you're not the one who needs to worry about paying your employees while in the other scenario you are in control of everything but with this comes the responsibility to manage it well as having other people depend on you. If you can't pay, they can't feed their family, if your boss or employer can't pay, you can't feed your family. The type of job or business type you decide to start will end up dictating how much growth you can have and the speed at which your income will be growing. You can't expect to be growing at massive rates if the business you have isn't scalable and has no reach.

Let's go back to our baby elephant example. If you are raising a baby elephant you can pretty much expect you will end up with an adult elephant but if what you have is a puppy then there is no way that puppy is going to end up being the size of an elephant, no matter how much time and effort you spend in raising him.

Another possibility is to get a job to finance your business or an investment. If this second stream of income grows enough for you to be able to leave your job without feeling it's too risky then you've reached your goal. Or to use it to fund and grow your passive income while you continue to work. It all depends on you. The difference with the traditional employee is that you go in having a way out.

Be aware of your taxes, you could be legally paying less than you currently are but make sure you pay them. The IRS is not an entity to mess with. Neither is the law, so make sure everything you're doing is legal, even if you earn millions they're not worth it if you don't get to enjoy them because you're inside a prison cell.

RENT VS BUY

Just because everyone is getting a house and a mortgage doesn't mean you have to get one. This might be a little difficult when you have the pressure from family and friends to get a house and settle down or whatever.

Is renting really a waste of money? Not really, but it depends on how you're using the money you'll be saving while renting. If you just plan to spend the extra $500 you're saving per month by living in a rental property then it would be smarter to buy the house as it will help as a way to preserve the value of the money. You do need to take into consideration that a house is not an investment if you're buying it to live in it. Think of it as a savings account. The money you put in it will help you buy the house and have a property. Every time you put money in it, it grows. While a house might not grow, it will increase in value, but it doesn't become an investment or an asset until you liquidate and receive the money or you move out and start renting it. Just like a savings account, if you are not using the money, it will not generate you money.

As a side note, you also need to ask yourself if you plan to continue living in the city you are at the moment. If you live in Florida but plan to move to California in the next 2 years it might make more sense to rent as you don't plan to stay long term and it is not like you can take the house with you.

Sometimes it is a lot cheaper to rent than it is to buy. Some landlords even lose money every month just by maintaining the properties they own and renting them at an accesible amount because otherwise they would be vacant and cost them even more money or they want the house for its future valuation and don't mind renting it at a lower price. So in any of these cases you would actually be living in a nicer house for a lot less than it would cost you to own the property.

However if you found yourself in a similar scenario as the 2008 one where they're selling houses for 1/3 of their real value and you happen to have the cash to buy it then go ahead and do so. It will probably go back to its original value in a few years and the banks are desperate to sell those properties to become liquid again. You need to be careful with this though, if you buy a house during an economic crisis and can only afford to hold it for 3 months it could be extremely dangerous as it can take two years for the economy to recover from a depression. Sometimes it takes more, sometimes less, in the end there's nothing that can accurately predict how fast or slow the economy will come back but it always will. Whatever goes up, must come back down and vice versa.

Now, one important topic to cover is if you can actually afford to buy a house. You need to be realistic and plan for the worst case scenario so that no unpleasant unknowns come up and take you by surprise. Take into consideration how much you make and if you have enough savings to do make a considerable downpayment. A higher downpayment (20% or more) will get you a lower payment on your debt because you don't have to pay for mortgage insurance. It can also get you approved for a higher loan so be careful with this. This doesn't mean you have to spend all of your savings in your downpayment, you should actually keep your savings such as your emergency fund and the 4-6 month fund for example.

Whether you rent or own, remember to include these expenses and all the other expenses that come with owning a house as extra costs into your monthly expenses. Additional costs such as taxes, maintenance, water, light and insurance are sometimes not considered before buying a house or signing a contract but they can end up making the property too expensive. Just because you can afford the mortgage doesn't mean you can afford the house. Imagine if you have to do a major repair and it costs $10,000, using up all your savings on the downpayment doesn't seem like the best idea anymore.

A similar scenario happens with cars. You can now lease cars, which is a nice option if you want a new car every two years or so but don't want to buy it and sell it that often. Or if you can't afford to buy one but still need one to go to work. Once again, just because you can afford the monthly payment doesn't mean you can afford the car, and if you're in a situation in which money is tight, do not go for a new model under the excuse that you need a reliable vehicle. There are plenty inexpensive reliable vehicles that you can get instead of a new model. When buying cars make sure you are taking into consideration all the costs that come with owning a car. It is not only the downpayment plus the monthly fee, you also need to take into consideration the gas, maintenance, insurance, repairs, oil changes, parking, etc, etc.

Going back to the topic of houses, investing in real estate is one of the best and preferred methods of investments there are. Make sure to look at properties that have a high chance of valuating but also that could generate you a profit from rent as soon as possible as well. These investments require more upfront capital than other ones and I'd suggest you talk to someone who knows about real estate in your area as well as a lawyer before investing in properties.

SAVINGS

Would you jump off a plane without a parachute on? I really hope you answered this question with a no. Lacking savings would be the equivalent of doing something risky such as jumping from a building without having a safety net. It might be a very short building but still, savings are your safety net. If an emergency happened, you can always count on your savings to help you cover it but what happens when you have no savings? You end up having to go into debt, even if the interest rates are extremely high you can't afford to say no. It is not like you have a choice, which is extremely dangerous because you're no longer in control of your situation. This scenario is less than ideal and could set you back a couple of years in your journey to financial freedom.

You should always aim to start your savings account or fund as soon as possible. The tricky part about savings is that you don't accidentally start saving in most cases. (It's not like "Oh no! I accidentally saved $4,000 again!") You actually need to do a conscious effort in order to start building a healthy savings account. I have found that when I keep money on my bank account I tend to spend it because I think it's available money, so what I did was to have a separate account for my savings. You can do this as well if you think you do this too. You can also keep your savings in a waterproof and fire-resistant safe at your home or somewhere else you consider safe.

You should always pay yourself first, which means that as soon as you get money you should put it away or set up an automatized way to transfer it to your savings account so that you don't even see it in your primary bank account.

How much you should have in savings depends entirely on you but some financial advisors recommend 4, 6 or even 8 months worth of expenses so that you can continue living the life you're living now in case you lost your job, suffered from an injury or there was an economic crisis. Personally I consider 6 months to be a good amount since it gives you enough time to find a solution without keeping too much of your money tied up. Remember this should cover your essentials such as rent and food, and since it's ultimately an emergency fund it's not like you should be adding expenses such as going to the movies or eating out at fancy restaurants.

For example, if you have a monthly budget of $2,500, then you would need to save 2,500 x 6 = **$15,000** in order to have enough to keep paying for your living expenses for 6 months if you were to find yourself without your primary source of income.

Apart from that fund you should have another one called the emergency fund. In this one you should keep enough money to cover an emergency, whatever it might be. It can range from $1,000 to $10,000 or however much you want. I would recommend starting with this fund as it is a smaller amount which you can save up pretty quickly for. Even if you currently live with your parents, it is never too soon to have an emergency fund, even if it is just $500.

One of the worst decisions I took when I was younger was to spend all my savings on traveling. While I don't regret the travels because they were amazing, it did put me at risk when adversity came. Believe me, it always comes and you better be prepared for it. I wasn't, and this set me back almost one whole year in my saving and investing goals but it also made me resourceful. So in the end, I learned a lot and I'm grateful it happened early and the consequences weren't serious because the bigger you grow, the harder the fall. However, I could have avoided all this trouble by having an emergency fund.

On the other side of the spectrum, there are activities which require us to save in order to be able to do them.

We're not talking about saving enough money for a rainy day but about saving for something we want to buy or do. Experiences, specially traveling to another country and experiencing its culture is one of the best feelings ever. This is perfect if you're a minimalist because when you travel, you make memories which will last you a lifetime without having to bring many items or buy stuff. Travel is quite expensive when you compare it to other recreational activities and it requires at least a few months of savings depending on where you're planning to go. If you want to go to Europe for 15 days and visit 3 countries then you will need to figure out how much it's going to cost and then start saving for the trip.

Airplane ticket: $1,250
Airbnb x 15 nights: $1,050
Food (lunch, dinner, snacks and coffee): $450
Transportation (train, flights between countries): $700
Tickets for museums and other activities: $350
Shopping and souvenirs: $0 (A minimalist remains a minimalist even when traveling!)
Unexpected expenses (even if you don't use it, it's better to have it): $200
TOTAL: **$4,000**

Now that you have the total amount you can start saving towards that goal in many different ways. I like to use the envelope system for this type of saving as it keeps the money out of sight and in a place in which I don't have easy access to but you can save in whatever way you find best. The envelope system as the name suggests, consists on putting money into an envelope and it's divided into specific categories. "Trip to Italy" or "gas money".

Savings are something you need but would be preferable to have only an optimal amount so that you're able to invest the rest and grow your income as an effect.

Necessary savings:
At least 4 months worth of expenses (could be 6 depending on what makes you feel more comfortable).
Emergency fund of at least $1,000.
Once you have these savings you should be ready to start saving to invest, for example saving your next $3,000 to start selling on Amazon FBA or to get $100 to **start your blog**.

Another option is to get a credit card with 0% interest. Yes, these exist but it's usually a technique banks use to acquire you as a customer and it only lasts around a year or so. While this wouldn't be my first choice when it comes to financing an emergency, 0% interest is a lot preferable than 30% interest. So try to look for this type of credit cards if having a credit card makes you feel more secure.

MAKING A BUDGET

Making a budget can turn out to be a bit difficult, specially if you've never done one before. The important step is to start, you will notice that once you start writing down your expenses and income, the other items will continue to flow into your mind. It doesn't need to be perfect from the start and you can always add or take out items.

In order to make a budget that adjusts to your lifestyle, you need to be aware of your goals. If you have absolutely no interest in having a savings account and you think it is completely useless then what would be the point of having a percentage dedicated to savings? Taking an example that's not as extreme as that one, if you don't own or need a car then it makes no sense to add it to your budget. However you do need to take into consideration how much you spend on transportation and add it under that category.

Analyze the data you have from previous months and work your way from there with the help of your goals. If you have literally no idea of where your money has gone in the past few months, you can ask the bank to send you a credit or debit card statement with everything you've spent your money on. While this might be a little painful to look at (specially if you spend a ton of money on useless things), it will also help you open up your eyes to what's going on with your financial situation.

Start by using your income as the first guideline.
Remember that your income needs to cover:
Expenses
Savings
Investments (or savings for investments)
Debt repayments
The amount you decide to give to each one of these categories depends entirely on you.

Once you have a tentative amount of how much money you want to spend on expenses monthly then you can start your budget.
First, add all of your necessary expenses which you can't avoid and definitely have to pay every month such as rent, car payments, gas, food, insurance, etc.
Now you will be left with some leftover money which you can use to spend in the things you want such as a new jacket or your morning coffees (which aren't essential but contribute to your overall level of happiness).

Once you take a closer look at what you're spending your money on you might want to change some of your habits, this new found money can either go to your savings or towards something that's more meaningful for you such as being able to afford going to the theatre every month or even fund your trading account to start trading in the stock market. Again, this is going to depend a lot on your goals because a person whose goal is to become an artist will spend his or her money in a different way than a person who wants to become a trader.

BUDGETING TOOLS AND TECHNIQUES

In the end it is about finding the one that works for you. There could be the most perfect system on earth for budgeting but if it doesn't fit you, you're not going to follow it, meaning you will end up where you started which is not paying attention to your finances.

Envelope system
This one is quite interesting and I wanted to try it out as it caught my attention. It consists on separating your money into different envelopes with different categories written on them such as "rent", "food", "gas", "savings", etc. The whole point of this exercise is to have a designated amount of money for each one of the envelopes and then only spend that. If you run out of money in one of the envelopes, you should "steal" from the others to fund that specific one. This will force you to accurately calculate how you're going to divide your money.

While I didn't end up using this system as my only system, I did end up applying it to my savings. If I want to save for a trip, a new phone or to save money I absolutely can't touch, I use envelopes.

The fun thing about envelopes is that you can write on them and keep count of how much you have on the inside. Each one of my envelopes is named with the goal I'm planning to achieve with it, the amount I need and an encouraging quote to save money that I read every time I see the envelope.

Excel

Pretty self explanatory, you put in your income and expenses and then calculate how much you're spending and if you have a positive number after subtracting your expenses from your income then you're good. Increasing that number will help you save more money per month.

The advantage of Excel is that you can have a format that you can copy and paste every month to calculate how you're doing. Plus, you don't need a calculator since you can put in the formula directly into the sheets.

This is the other method I use since it's so simple and you can lock the document with a password so that only you can look at it.

Excel is hands down my favorite method as it's the simplest and it helps you keep track of everything by simplifying the processes.

Apps

There are some great budgeting apps out there that connect automatically with your credit and debit cards so that you can see an organized summary of how you're spending your money. Some of these are Mint, You Need a Budget and Wally.

70/20/10

If you have read the book The Richest Man in Babylon, this will sound familiar to you. In that book, the author recommends that you use 70% for your expenses (in here is included your clothes and any other luxury you might want to give yourself), 20% to pay off any debts you have and 10% to save. The catch is that you save up to the point in which you can invest that money. Remember, only invest in that which you're familiar with or that you know about. Investments become an expense if you end up losing that money.

50/30/20

Fairly similar to the 70/20/10, but in this one you spend 50% on necessities such as rent, heating and food, 30% on wants such as clothes or cable and 20% on savings and debt repayment.

Whatever you choose, just make sure to be consistent with it and to not use incorrect data, as the only person you will be lying to is yourself.
Use a system which works with your personality type, if you need to be reminded in order to fill in the input of your monthly expenses, set an alarm on your phone

every 5th of the month and have the document in which you keep your budget easily accesible.

SMART BUDGET

In order to have a smart budget, you need to know how much you're spending and exactly where is your money going each month. You don't have to track it every single month as you might go crazy writing down every single gum packet but you will have an idea of where your money is going and how to manage it before you spend it. Instead of writing down $1.50 for coffee every single month, just calculate how much you spend in coffee and other food in general and assign that to your food category. This will save you the step of including your morning coffee expense every single day having an average of how many coffees you drink multiplied by how many days you usually get coffee. While this might not be the most accurate method, it will save you a ton of time which you can use for other activities, whether they are income-generating activities or just quality time you spend with loved ones.

A smart budget is a way for you to easily assess where your money is going and know how much you have available to save and spend. It is a way of turning a "boring" budgeting technique into something you can use every single month and understand it completely in just 5 minutes. It doesn't demand your time and everything has been automatized. The result? Easily trackable finances.

A smart budget takes as a premise that you are looking to generate more money, live below your means and increase your assets. While at the same time reduce high interest debt and pay off loans.

Summarized:

INCOME

Increase this, preferably by acquiring assets that generate you another stream of income every month. Increasing your income will also increase your capacity to acquire more assets, therefore making your income grow exponentially rather than linearly as it would with a normal job.

The secret to keeping this part as simple as possible is to take time to create an Excel sheet and include all the sources from which you're receiving money. If you need to add a new source you can just add a new row and Excel will sum it automatically while keeping the formulas in every cell.

Income Sources Example

Job 9-5 (could be Job half-time)	$1,800
Freelancing	$150
Youtube	$120
Stock photos	$0.25

eBook royalties	$77
Income Total	$2,147.25

EXPENSES

Decrease this if possible or if you're spending more per month than what you're earning. One easy way to reduce your expenses is to cut everything out that's not useful for you or that's not contributing to your happiness or wellbeing. If your income increases make sure your expenses don't go up in the same percentage. The easiest thing to do is to automate those payments which are necessary as well as the contributions to your savings/investments accounts.

Expenses Example

Rent (automated)	- $800
Utilities (automated)	(included)
Food	- $200
Eating out/ Coffee	-$130
Car Payment	- $180
Gas	- $120
Car insurance	- $60
Entertainment	- $60
Expenses Total	-$1,550

TOTAL: INCOME - EXPENSES: $597.25

As you can see in this example, your income exceeds your expenses. This is good as you can use what's left to save or invest.

If your total was negative, then you need to find a way to make it positive as having a negative total will make you go into debt because you're spending more per month than what you're earning.

Now, I want you think about your financial situation as if it were a company or a business. Apart from the income you receive and the expenses you have to incur in, companies have assets and liabilities. This isn't that different from our finances work.

ASSETS

Assets hold value and sometimes put money in your pocket every single month, so it is a great idea to acquire and grow them.

Car	$5,000
Jewellery	$500
Stocks	$2,000
Cash	$990
Total	$8,490

LIABILITIES

Liabilities are everything that you owe and they take money from you, decrease them unless they add to your overall wellbeing and happiness.

Car loan	- $2,800
Credit card debt	- $1,800

| Total | - $4,600 |

NET WORTH

Another number you should be aware of is your net worth, this is the sum of what you own versus what you owe and it helps you understand where you are financially.

NET WORTH: ASSETS - LIABILITIES: $8,490 - $4,600
TOTAL NET WORTH: $3,890

Being in debt will set you back by a lot since that money that you owe is moving your net worth towards red numbers. Just as with the budget, you should aim to have a positive net worth.

WEALTH IS AN ILLUSION

What would you do if I told you that you could be living the lifestyle of the rich right now? And that most people who are living luxury lifestyles are actually broke or in debt? You have to be careful with the people who you admire and wish you had their lives as most people go into debt in order to finance that lifestyle. Even if you make $250,000 per year and you're spending $275,000 you are actually worth less (financially speaking, aka net worth) than someone who is making $50,000 per year but saving half of it and has no debt. However, as a high earner you have the advantage that just by switching you habits you can end up saving a lot more in a much shorter time frame than the person who's just earning $50,000.

Let's look at an example:

Derek is young and works as a hotel manager and **makes $ 50,000 after taxes**, however he still lives with his parents and isn't married or has children. **Monthly income after tax: $ 4,167** aprox.

Bruce is a senior data engineer and **makes $ 150,000 per year after taxes**, he has 3 children and is married to Angela who decided to quit her job in order to take care of their children (If you are a feminist and would rather have Angela be the senior data engineer then by all means imagine it that way). **Monthly income after tax: $ 12,500** aprox.

Since Derek lives with his parents, he has no expenses apart from his phone bill ($60) and he offered to help with the electricity bill ($112) to help his family. He lives in the suburbs in a small house that his parents bought when they got married. He likes going out with his friends once a week to a nice restaurant ($400) and also enjoys going clubbing every week ($550). Apart from that, he buys coffee ($90) in the morning and he has lunch ($357) at work everyday since his break isn't long enough for him to go back to his house. He saves the rest of his income because he wants to travel the world and start investing.

Derek's expenses per month: $ 1,569
Derek's savings per month: $ 2,598
Derek's projected savings per year: $ 31,176

Bruce's situation is a little different, he has to pay rent on a 5 bedroom house which is $4,050 per month plus every expense that comes with owning a house like the electricity bill ($180), water is included unless they go over their water allowance, everyone in the house apart from their younger daughter has a phone ($60 x 4 = $ 240) and they also have to pay their internet bill ($100), cable ($120) and organic food ($1,600).

He also has a car loan for his new car ($600) and his wife's ($450) for both of which he has to pay car insurance ($180).

2 of his sons are in high school and go to a private school ($1,735.50) and his daughter goes to preschool ($416).

Other expenses include new clothes every month for everyone in the family ($600) and Angela has a taste for designer handbags and other goods ($450).

Bruce also decided to take his family on a vacation to Italy for the kids to meet their uncles and aunts since Angela is Italian and wanted to visit her family, since he has a high interest credit card he decided to pay at least $2,000 per month.

Bruce's expenses per month: $ 12,721.50
Bruce's deficit per month: -$ 221.50
Bruce's projected deficit per year: -$ 2,658

It's better to be rich than to look rich. Most "rich" people are in debt anyway because they need to finance a high level of living to keep appearances. This problem arises when you haven't earned the lifestyle you're living. As you can see from the previous example, it didn't matter that Bruce was making almost 3 times more than Derek because he had such high expenses that he ended up spending more money than what he made. Eventually, Derek's savings could be used to buy a rental property that makes him semi passive income, allowing him to retire earlier. However, if Bruce realizes he's living a dangerous lifestyle that's only drowning him and his family in debt and makes a conscious effort to change it then he might be able to do the same.

Earn it first, then live it. You will realize what you thought you wanted in the first place isn't what you really wanted but more of a social construct of what we're supposed to have by a certain age. Try not to feel pressured by others to take a job you hate and that you feel is basically killing you just because it's an "amazing opportunity".

There is also a secret to luxury living that most people don't realize and it's that you can live like a millionaire without actually earning like one. There are many countries in which the cost of living is a lot lower than in the U.S., meaning that by earning the same income you could be living like a king in those countries. There is a city in Guatemala called Antigua which has a high percentage of house owners who are retired Americans. Want to take a guess why that is? Well, apart from being a beautiful city it is also very cheap in comparison to America, meaning that if you retired and got those payments every month even if it wasn't enough to sustain the level that you had in Chicago, you could still afford to live comfortably for years to come in Antigua. However if you came from one of the neighboring cities in Guatemala which are cheaper than Antigua, you would probably have a hard time sustaining a living there, even if you're working full time on that other city or town. What can we get out of this information? That it is preferable to earn a high income and live below your means, whether that means working remotely and living in a cheaper location such as Thailand, which has stunning views. Or even moving to a cheaper location within your country or city or reducing your expenses and living below your means in whatever location you might be.

YOUR STARTING POINT DOESN'T DETERMINE YOUR OUTCOME

Remember the baby elephant? Well, we all start somewhere. It doesn't matter if you barely graduated from high school and didn't finish university. Eventually, the people who keep putting in the hours and effort in the right place will end up being rewarded for the value they provided. This also means that even if you started out as privileged, that isn't a guarantee you'll continue to live that way.

If you're one of those people who did well in school and got a comfortable job you need to be even more careful because you will be in a position from which you have no external pressure or motivation to get out of. You're not struggling. You could just comfortably stay there forever without any apparent consequences. Of course this isn't a bad thing if you enjoy your job and wouldn't mind staying in the same company for a few years until you eventually move to a higher position. Just remember to save money for your retirement and invest when good opportunities present themselves.

Most people live paycheck to paycheck without worrying much about the future. This is a very dangerous position to be in. Imagine being in a city that's about to be hit by a tsunami, except you don't know the tsunami it's coming until it hits. The tsunami can be anything from losing your job, to an economic recession (think 2008) to becoming sick and not being able to work for a prolonged period of time. The problem is that you planned for the best case scenario but didn't prepare for the worse and if anything worse than ideal happens, then prepare for a tough year following that.

I have seen people who started their lives sleeping in a cardboard box on the streets (true story) and ended up being one of the richest families in the country just like I have seen wealthy families lose everything they had in just a couple of years due to bad financial decisions and substance abuse. Both situations are impressive and I'm sure you wouldn't have guessed the futures of these people if you had seen them in their early stages.

What I'm trying to say with this is that it doesn't matter where you are in this moment, what matters the most is what you decide to do and what you do with your time every single day. Success habits are formed with the actions we take daily. You can't just expect to wake up one morning and miraculously be super productive, sit down and write the novel you've been wanting to write for years in 4 hours non stop just as you can't expect to wake up one morning and bench 200 pounds if you've never been to a gym. If you have big plans, start by setting small, achievable goals. If you want to bench 200 pounds you can start by lifting 10 and then working your way up. Even if you started out by not being able to lift even 20 pounds, once you put in consistent effort you will eventually get there (or at least to 100 pounds).

There are some traits that successful people have in common. Being smart enough to develop them and seeing the change they make in our lives is life changing. If you're living like a successful person, it is only a matter of time for success to catch up to you. And I'm not talking posting pictures on social media of you with $100 bills and in front of luxury cars. I'm talking about putting in the effort everyday without seeking admiration or motivation from external sources. Working silently will prevent you from being distracted and haters won't know what to attack.

Wake up early to get stuff done before everyone else wakes up.

Have clear, defined goals with an action plan you can follow everyday.

And seek to add value, not to make money, and the money will come.

DEALING WITH EXTERNAL PRESSURE

You might have to deal with some pressure from family, friends or even your significant other. Resistance to change is common and the best way to deal with it is to show the benefits from the results.

Dealing with external pressure is a lot easier if the pressure comes from people with whom you only associate a few hours every day or see only once a week.
You can tell them that you would like them to respect your decision to be a minimalist and would prefer if they didn't comment negatively on it but if they have any questions or would like to talk about your lifestyle that you're available and open to that. Remember most critics come from lack of understanding of your situation.

Of course, it is hard if everyone is pressuring you to buy a house, a car, get married and have kids. It becomes even more difficult if you live with these people. Whether they are your parents, siblings or partner, your decisions might affect them as well, specially if you're married and you are the one in control of the finances in your house since a bad financial decision could have a negative impact in the way you both live.

If you want them to understand your decision, show them the benefits of this lifestyle. If you don't have a record of how this works then you can make a projection using your current income and expenses and another one using your future income and expenses.

How's it going to look in one year? What about 5 or 10? Bigger numbers cause a greater impact and if you tell your partner you could be saving $15,000 per year just by reducing a few expenses then I'm sure they'll be on board. You can also use this as motivation so out of the amount that you plan to save you can designate a percentage such as 50% which you can use to travel somewhere you've always wanted to go to or to try out new restaurants and experiences in the area. At the same time you will be saving the other 50% for a long term goal or using some of it to invest.

SOME MONEY LESSONS I'VE LEARNED OVER THE YEARS

These are some money lessons I've learned over the years either by personal experience or by listening to other people's journeys.

The time to sell is when someone is buying and viceversa, the time to buy it's when something is on sale. You will most likely be able to sell at a higher price and you don't have to take the time it takes to sell the item into consideration either, while if you're in a situation in which everyone is selling their stuff but no one is buying, you'll get a better price.

Cash is king. Being liquid is one of the biggest advantages you can have as an investor, specially during a time of economic crisis. One of my friends' dad was able to buy an apartment 20% below market price just because he had the available funds in his bank account. I must add however that he is also an avid negotiator and real estate developer as well, it wasn't like he just walked in and demanded a 20% discount. Work on your negotiation skills.

If everyone's doing it, then it's most likely a bubble. Everyone knows about it, everyone is talking about it and everyone is learning how to earn money that way (and they are making money). These are signs that you should stay away from this opportunity unless you're going to bet against it. Take the Bitcoin bubble as an example, when it passed the $8,000 mark, everyone was crazy getting into the trend and buying Bitcoin. Then it reached a top price of almost $20,000 only to go crashing down to $5,500 and stabilizing at around $6,500. I'm not saying Bitcoin is a scam or anything like that, but in this example you can clearly see what a bubble looks like before, during and after it pops. The price might even go up to $20,000 again in the future if it becomes an acceptable medium of exchange but for now, its real value is around $6,500. Here you can see a chart on how the **price of Bitcoin has behaved in the past**.

It is better to be the owner of a small thing than one replaceable part in a system. Meaning it is a lot better to own your own business than to be an employee. Why? Because if you're an employee, you instantly become replaceable. When you're the owner of the business, the only way you're replaced is if you decide to hire someone to take your place. However, being an employee it is a great way to learn how the business operates at other levels and to gain experience in the industry.

I'm by no means hating on having a job, there are some people who are a perfect fit for the employee profile and they're just as valuable to the organization as everyone else because it needs them to continue functioning correctly. Just don't rely entirely on a job, start saving and investing as soon as possible.

It's better to have 10% of a huge cake than it is to have 100% of a cupcake. Meaning if you can partner up with people who can make your business grow, it's a lot better than remaining the only owner of a small business that will probably never generate too much. If I can make $100 per month by selling my course on my own but I could make $1,000 if I join forces with someone looking to promote my content for 50% commission then it's a lot better for both of us to start a partnership.

Money gets bored. If you're not using your money and it is sitting there in your bank account or safe, it's most likely going to get bored. Money wants movement, it wants to work for you and make you more money. Why are you keeping it prisoner? It will eventually find a way to escape, usually through illogical purchases or expensive experiences.

Earning money is half the battle. Keeping it is the other half. People think that the hardest part about becoming rich is to get the money, however this is just half of the equation. You need to learn how to properly manage money if you want to get rich.

Be nice to everyone and try to not get into fights. What has this got to do with money? Everything, money (or wealth) is cyclical, and if you go around picking fights with everyone when you're at the top, you'll most likely have to come back begging for them to give you an opportunity when you're at the bottom. It is a lot easier to have friends than to keep enemies. You never know when you're going to need someone's help.

Consistency is the key to success. If you stay consistent and work on one opportunity, you're many times more likely to become successful than someone who jumps from opportunity to opportunity and never achieves anything.

Those are some of the most valuable lessons I've learned throughout the years. If you liked this book and found it valuable, please leave a review with your thoughts on it. It is extremely helpful and I'll be eternally grateful.

Without further do, let's jump to the last bit.

CONCLUSION

In the end, the only person who is responsible for your life and financial future is yourself and you should be actively participating in how it's turning out. If you see it's going a way you don't particularly like you have the power to change it into whatever it is you want.

The basic lessons I want you to take from this book are:

- Increase your passive income. This will provide you with the freedom to do whatever you like. You will be in total control of your income and time.
- Live below your means. There is no way to acquire wealth if you spend more than what you earn.
- Acquire assets. Assets will generate you money and hold value.
- Reduce Liabilities. Being in debt isn't fun, pay off your debts as soon as possible.
- Learn how to manage money. Earning money is half the battle, you need to learn how to manage it so that you start saving and investing, otherwise it'll just pass through your bank account.
- Acquire valuable skills. Even if you lose everything, you'll still have your skills so acquire ones that are valuable.

- Dream big and work hard. The only limits you have are the ones you set for yourself. Be brave enough to set big goals and then work everyday towards achieving them.
- Debt can be good if you're using it to generate more money but it can be devastating if you have to go into debt and pay a high interest rate.
- Whether you decide to start a business or work at a job, make sure to build a second and even third stream of income because you can never be 100% certain of how the future is going to turn out.
- There are plenty of ways to make money, but once you choose one you should be consistent and loyal to it until it can walk by itself and continue generating money without depending on you.

Remember that even elephants start small, we all start somewhere, decide you you want to become.

RESOURCES

Here's a table of the resources that are included in the book:

Blogging with Bluehost
Start your own Wordpress blog for only $3.95 per month with a free domain included by using this link.

Fiverr
Hire freelancers to help you with tasks such as writing, editing, covers, proof-reading, translation and anything else you might think of.

Airbnb
Rent your own property or look at properties to stay at while traveling. Airbnb gives you the option to turn your liability into an asset and to find somewhere to stay when you travel that you absolutely love and is in the perfect location.

Shutterstock
Shutterstock lets you monetize the beautiful photos you take by providing you with a platform to upload them and receive a commission every time someone downloads them.

Amazon KDP

Start selling your own books on Amazon and reaching a worldwide audience.

Amazon FBA

Start selling items from anywhere in the world in the market you choose. Make sure you follow all the guidelines for products that Amazon provides you with and to do a market analysis to test demand before investing in a product.

Alibaba

This is the site in which you can communicate with providers in Asia if you want to outsource items to sell in your country.

Robinhood

This is the best option if you want to start trading and live in the U.S. since they don't charge for commissions and the platform is super friendly.

IQ Option

If you live outside of the USA, Russia, Canada, Australia, Belgium, Latvia, Japan, Turkey, Israel, Syria, Sudan and Iran, check out this option if you want to start trading. Take into consideration that there are no guarantees to make money if you trade and you might even lose money sometimes.

Make sure to do your own research before investing. Remember that not all investments are profitable and that you might even lose money when investing. The best thing you can do is to talk to an expert in the field, a financial advisor, and a lawyer as well as to educate yourself in the topic so that you have complete understanding of the opportunity you're about to take.